# Your Core Reading Program & Children's Literature

## Effective Strategies for Using the Best of Both

## Diane Barone & Suzette Youngs

## SCHOLASTIC

New York • Toronto • London • Auckland • Sydney
Mexico City • New Delhi • Hong Kong • Buenos Aires

Credit: "The Dream Keeper," from THE COLLECTED POEMS OF LANGSTON HUGHES by Langston Hughes, edited by Arnold Rampersad with David Roessel, Associate Editor, copyright © 1994 by The Estate of Langston Hughes. Used by permission of Alfred A. Knopf, a division of Random House, Inc.

Cover design: Brian LaRossa
Interior design: LDL Designs
Acquiring Editor: Lois Bridges
Production Editor: Dana Truby
Copy Editor: Erich Strom

ISBN-13: 978-0-545-04708-4
ISBN-10: 0-545-04708-0

# Dedication

*The dedication of this book could only belong to one person—our editor, Lois Bridges. Not long ago, we were attending a national reading conference, waiting in the lobby for sessions to begin, when who should we meet but Lois. In the space of ten minutes, Lois had convinced us to write this book and its companion. Along the way, she encouraged us in our writing endeavor, supported us, read preliminary drafts, and so much more. For her nudging, support, and friendship we dedicate this book to her.*

# $C$ontents

CHAPTER 1

# *U*sing the Best of Both: Why Combining a Core Reading Program and a Literature-Based Approach Works

*Teachers are architects who design much more than the appearance of their class-rooms. They establish its underlying composition—its character, its temperament, its intentions, its goals. Teachers, too, must be versatile—part artist, part architect, part poet, part philosopher, part supportive advocate, part demanding taskmaster—dreamers and doers all at once.*

—Margaret Stewart (2002)

We chose this quote to begin *Your Core Reading Program & Children's Literature: Effective Strategies for Using the Best of Both: 4–6* because it describes what we believe to be a unique way to view teachers—as architects. Stewart understands the flexibility and structure you, as a teacher, must provide to meet the learning needs of your students. The metaphor "architect of learning" creates an opportunity for you to see yourself as a creator of learning possibilities. Using the creative and scientific aspects of teaching literacy as your raw materials, we see you expanding your schedules, materials, and teaching strategies to include multiple opportunities for providing effective instruction to students. You will move from being a teacher who follows a template to an inspired teacher who creates it. Throughout this book, we build on this metaphor through suggestions and supportive strategies to simultaneously use a core reading program and a literature-based curriculum to enrich students' literacy growth and motivation to read and write.

We worry that so many teachers feel disheartened with the ways they currently teach children to read and write. You may be expected to teach a core reading program to students for 90 minutes a day and feel that limits how you might teach reading. You may also be expected to teach test-taking strategies, usually a given in the current high-stakes environment, and feel that this limits the time left for other curricular goals. You may perceive that the art and craft of teaching have moved to the background of your instruction and the science of teaching reading and writing and test preparation has moved to the foreground.

Recently, we have all been inundated with the science of reading instruction. The National Reading Panel (2000), the RAND Reading Study Group (2001), and the National Research Council report titled *Preventing Reading Difficulties in Young Children* (Snow, Burns, & Griffin, 1998) have provided much of the foundation for the scientific view of literacy instruction, especially in reading. Based on the results of the National Assessment of Educational Progress (NAEP), the national test of fourth, eighth, and twelfth graders, we have learned that this scientific base may not have been used effectively in the past and perhaps is not being effectively used right now in instruction in intermediate classrooms. Over the past 35 years, NAEP has provided an independent measure of what students across the United States know and can do in reading, mathematics, science, writing, and other core subject areas, and it has come to be known as "the nation's report card" (National Center for Education Statistics [NCES], 2007). Some of the general results reported in 2007 follow:

- In 2007, fourth graders scored higher in reading comprehension than in any previous year, with an average score of 221. (Scores range from 0 to 500.) Fourth graders also scored higher in literacy experiences (223) and reading for information (219).
- Higher reading scores were demonstrated for lower- and middle-performing students (in the 10th, 25th, and 50th percentiles).
- The percentage of fourth graders performing at or above Basic increased to 67 percent. The Proficient group increased to 33 percent.
- Fourth-grade girls outperformed boys in reading. Girls' average score was 224 and boys' was 218.
- Black students' average reading scores were higher in 2007 than in 1992 (203, up from 192).
- Hispanic students' average reading scores were higher in 2007 than in 1992 (205, up from 197) (http://nces.ed.gov/nationsreportcard).

NAEP uses its own unique reading-performance-level descriptions. Understanding them is important because NAEP expects sophisticated performance from students. Although often it may sound, from the performance level title, that students did not do particularly well, in fact their performance was satisfactory—for instance, the Basic level students comprehended the text passages presented to them. This is not to say that teachers would not want to see more students achieve at the Proficient or Advanced levels. As teachers we need to understand what is expected on this test, or we may believe that students in the fourth grade performed more poorly than they actually did. While we may feel frustrated by NAEP results, the evidence is that students are doing better than they have in the past, and this is happening at a time when classrooms are becoming increasingly diversified (Hannaway, Fix, & Passel, 2004). Following are descriptions of levels of performance for the reading portion of the test.

- **Basic**—Fourth-grade students performing at the Basic level demonstrate an understanding of the overall meaning of what they read. When reading text appropriate for fourth graders, they make relatively obvious connections between the text and their own experiences and extend the ideas in the text by making simple inferences.
- **Proficient**—Fourth-grade students performing at the Proficient level demonstrate an overall understanding of the text, providing inferential as well as literal information. When reading text appropriate to fourth grade, they extend the ideas in the text by making inferences, drawing conclusions, and making connections to their own experiences. The connection between the text and what the student infers are clear.
- **Advanced**—Fourth-grade students performing at the Advanced level generalize about topics in the reading selection and demonstrate an awareness of how authors compose and use literary devices. When reading text appropriate to fourth grade, they judge text critically and, in general, give thorough answers that indicate careful thought.

For more information about NAEP, you can visit http://nces.ed.gov/nationsreportcard. There are also sample questions that you may be interested in exploring with your students.

High-stakes assessments such as NAEP and those required by the No Child Left Behind Act to determine schools' adequate yearly progress (AYP) have changed teaching and learning environments. In elementary schools, these changes are particularly apparent in intermediate classrooms, where the effectiveness of schools is measured through standardized assessments. As a result, more schools have been selecting core reading programs to assure that students have a systematic literacy curriculum throughout their elementary experience. Even in the current high-stakes environment, we are optimistic that the best teaching and learning of literacy can be achieved through the use of both core reading programs and literature-based curricula. Okay, we see those folded arms and skeptical looks. We hear you saying, "Are you kidding? We only have time to do one, so we do what is mandated—there is no time for anything else!" We are asking—and this is a huge request—that you suspend your disbelief for the first few pages of this book . . . well, maybe for more than a few. So hang in there with us and critically review our arguments for the use of both, and reflect on the practical suggestions we share in Chapters 2, 3, and 4. Then take the time necessary to make a decision about the value of using both in your classroom and the ways in which you might have to rethink your organization, materials, and learning activities to support student learning through this approach. We are confident that you will recognize the advantages for your students and for yourself. In fact, we hope this book will help you reenergize your teaching of reading and writing.

There is no doubt that the science of teaching reading is important. It fosters more effective instruction in classrooms—instruction whose effectiveness has been documented. The science of reading has helped us to understand the importance of vocabulary and fluency instruction, for example. But the science of reading is just one part of literacy instruction and learning. Equally balanced with the science of teaching is the art of teaching. For instance, the art of teaching is demonstrated when you sit next to a student and support tentative understandings. Or when you recognize that students need more time to discuss a complex event that they read about in a social studies or science text. Or when you understand that your students' curiosity and creativity must be supported and extended through additional reading and writing. We see the art of teaching as the joyful part, the part that is full of possibilities. We see the science of teaching as the systematic part of literacy instruction, the part that supports the critical elements (phonological awareness, phonics, comprehension, vocabulary, and fluency) necessary for reading and writing success. Drawing on the teacher-as-architect metaphor again, these are the elements necessary for a structure to exist. The art of literacy instruction centers on extending the critical elements of literacy and focusing on the subtleties of instruction that facilitate student engagement and motivation—for an architect, this portion is the design of the structure. Exemplary literacy instruction is the amalgamation of the science and art of teaching. Such instruction supports students' literacy growth and students' enjoyment of reading and writing.

The tricky part is that the art and science of teaching cannot be separated into the art (literature-based) portion of the day and the science (core reading program) portion of the day. If only it were so simple. Instead, we offer ways to integrate the science part of literacy instruction into literature-based curricula and the art part into the core reading program. In our discussion, there is a blending of these two critical elements so that no instructional time is devoid of either one.

As you read this book, we hope you will think about the joy of learning and teaching. We hope you will visualize the pleasure in learning something new or in teaching a new concept to a student. Borrowing the words of Regie Routman, we hope you will ponder:

> "What am I doing to ensure that kids are joyful about reading and writing? What am I doing for myself to make my own life richer? There is no joy in assembly-line teaching nor in hours spent on test preparation, seatwork, or grading papers. If we are to create a thirst for knowledge and learning in our students and ourselves, we must put the joy back into our lives, savor the small victories, cheer our students on, and be unwavering advocates for them. Do whatever you need to do to guarantee that each and every student not only can learn but also savors learning" (2003, p. 221).

This book is written to help you balance the science and art of teaching so that you may once again savor learning and revel in the joyful moments of teaching.

This chapter establishes the foundation for using both. It begins with a discussion of effective literacy practices for teachers of intermediate students. We then present a discussion of the pros and cons of using core reading programs and literature-based curricula. We conclude the chapter with a discussion of the pragmatic issues related to using both in intermediate classrooms.

# Exemplary Literacy Instruction in the Intermediate Grades

The intermediate grades present special challenges for the literacy teacher. In the primary grades, learning to read is very visible. Students come to know the sounds of letters, and once they have discovered the alphabetic principle, they begin to decode simple consonant-vowel-consonant words like *dog*. From there, they move into reading more extended texts and focusing on comprehension, fluency, and vocabulary. As a result, learning becomes subtler and less transparent (Bear & Barone, 1998).

Most intermediate students prefer to read silently and are more fluent and flexible in their approach to reading and writing. They are aware of many genres and often have preferences for one or another. They also know that different genres expect different kinds of reading. In narrative text, it is fine to read quickly and even skim some pages. In informational text, each word becomes more important, and it is often necessary to slow down for effective comprehension (Barone, Mallette, & Xu, 2005; Bear & Barone, 1998).

Among other important changes that intermediate students experience are these:

1. **The books they read and the texts they write are longer.** They learn to sustain reading or writing over several days or weeks. Students may feel frustration as they try (and sometimes fail) to write a longer text that incorporates all the essential parts, such as a rich plotline, and they need the support of teachers to continue. Students acquire persistence as they begin to read novels or lengthy informational text, moving from single episodes of reading and writing to more sustained ones.

2. **Students consolidate early reading and writing behaviors.** They develop fluency in silent reading and can expend more mental energy on comprehension as they read through a text on the first encounter. The consolidation process requires that students have time to read and write. This is a time when they often prefer series books, in which the characters remain the same and the plot is the only element that varies. These books offer students the practice that they need to extend their reading proficiency.

3. **Students' understanding of words becomes much more flexible.** While most consonant-vowel-consonant words can be decoded from left to right, long vowel words cannot. For instance, with the word *cake*, students begin with initial consonant c and then must move to the end of the word to determine that the *e* changes the first vowel sound to a long *a*. Rather than a straight left-to-right process, there is a left-to-right sweep and then a return to the beginning to decode the word. Students engage in this process automatically and most do not realize that it is necessary to decode long-vowel words. Students also come to know the multiple meanings of single words like *run* or *bat*.

4. **Students respond to text more flexibly.** They might write retellings, summaries, or more analytical responses such as personal connections or thematic explorations (Barone, 1992).

All of these behaviors rely on incremental improvements in their literacy development. The move from picture books to chapter books is observable, but their ease or difficulty in comprehension may not be. Whether their reading rate is 120 words per minute or 90 may go unnoticed unless fluency is an important part of instruction. Teachers, students, and parents may not be aware of this growth unless it is made explicit for them. It's especially important for students to be made aware of their development as readers and writers. Otherwise, they may also be remiss in identifying themselves as more competent readers and writers, which can decrease their motivation. And motivation for intermediate students is critical. Research shows that students' motivation decreases each year they move through school (Dillon, 2005). Moreover, after fourth grade, boys fall behind girls in reading. Their frustration with reading only increases as the text levels grow more complex and the teacher's expectations grow higher (Newkirk, 2003).

While this book focuses primarily on instructional opportunities, these examples are just possibilities until skillful teachers, like you, enact them. Gambrell, Morrow, and Pressley (2007) identify several critical characteristics of highly effective teachers:

- Effective teachers work in school environments that are committed to improving student achievement. They work together to discuss and refine instruction that enhances student growth and development.
- Effective teachers behave like coaches. They support students in gaining meaning and often work next to them as they read or write.
- Effective teachers use higher-level responses to text. They use more authentic activities in supporting students' reading and writing. They manage multiple groupings of students.
- Effective teachers provide access to a multitude of books and time to engage with them.

Building on these attributes, Allington and Johnston studied outstanding fourth-grade teachers. They discovered that "excellent fourth-grade classrooms are constructivist, with students and teachers working *together*" (2002, p. xiii). They expand on this idea to acknowledge the collaborative working relationships between students and teachers in interpreting text to arrive at meaning. Such relationships are critical to student growth.

Whatever materials are available, we know that exemplary intermediate teachers can use them in flexible ways that support students to develop their abilities to read and write with meaning. You know how to directly teach the fundamental elements of literacy so that students can engage in rich oral and written discussions about text in collaborative settings with one another and their teacher. Simultaneously, you know how to extend students' reading and writing competencies so that they enjoy and pursue further reading and writing opportunities.

# Core Reading Programs

Searfoss, Readence, and Mallette (2001) write that no published program can by itself teach children to read. At the heart of the term *basal reading programs*, they write, is the word *basal*, which means "base," and so these materials should serve as a base, not as a total program. Basals and core reading programs have been available to teachers in this country for much of its history. Hoffman et al. (1998) observed that the first basal series, the McGuffey Readers, were used by teachers in the 1800s. Since then, publishing companies have been producing and continually revising core reading programs in response to the latest scientific evidence on reading instruction and learning. For instance, in the 1930s, reading programs had text selections that were written using a controlled vocabulary. When these controlled texts came under criticism, publishers included more text that included words based on their sound-symbol relationships (Popp, 1975). In the 1970s, reading programs were organized according to skills, with accompanying charts to check off each child's mastery of them. In response to criticism of that approach, publishers in the 1980s and 1990s devised reading programs that included more authentic children's literature. Today's core reading programs include authentic children's literature that consists of a variety of genres, with a heavier emphasis on informational text at all grade levels. They offer teachers a full language arts curriculum with emphasis on reading and all of its key elements—language, writing, and assessment materials. There is also greater emphasis on differentiated instruction. Leveled readers are provided to support the reading needs of students above, at, and below grade level.

We believe there are several reasons core reading programs have enjoyed such a long history in our schools. First of all, principals and school districts favor their use because it's convenient and cost effective—they can limit their purchases to a single full set of materials (Lapp, Fisher, Flood, Goss-Moore, & Moore, 2002).

Second, one way school districts have tried to improve student achievement is by adopting a core reading program. They want a systematic program that builds on previously taught skills and strategies throughout a school year and from year to year. By sanctioning and supporting core reading programs they can expect continuity in literacy instruction across schools within their district.

Third, teachers come and go. They may retire, move to another grade level, move to a new school, or choose another career. As a result, even with extensive professional development opportunities within a district or school, not all teachers will have participated. So if a literacy curriculum is based on an individual teacher's talents and expectations, there will be great variability from one class to another and from one year to the next. Though in some situations children may benefit from the strengths of an individual teacher's curriculum, most of the time the result will be a fractured literacy curriculum. For example, in a classroom led by a strong writing teacher, children develop into capable writers. However, a less well-prepared teacher may avoid this instruction altogether or just focus on low-level editing issues. Through the use of a core reading program, all teachers have sufficient guidance and materials to provide comprehensive reading instruction for students at a variety of reading levels, from the first to the last day of school.

Fourth, in many districts and schools, students move frequently. At one school in our community, the transiency rate is about 50 percent. Having a core reading program offers consistent instruction for such students. Schools use similar materials, and the organization of whole-group, small-group, and independent activity time is familiar. A consistent curriculum frees up students' attention so they can adjust to a new teacher, school, and classmates.

Finally, the use of a core reading program provides numerous opportunities for teachers to collaborate. They might discuss how best to share the core anthology literature selection with the class, how best to work with small groups, or how best to differentiate independent activities. They can decide how to use paraprofessionals to support students, perhaps in preteaching or reteaching activities. They can use common assessments to evaluate student learning, in order to plan for strategic instruction that best supports them. They can work together to improve questions offered in the teacher's edition, or on other aspects of the core reading program.

As you likely already know, core reading programs also receive their share of criticism. Most often, teachers complain that they have lost their freedom to teach in ways that are more satisfying to them (Hoffman et al., 1998). This lack of freedom is certainly real. Though exemplary teaching practices are part of a core reading program, selection of text, strategy focus, vocabulary, and so on are determined by the series publisher and authors. A similar criticism suggests that core reading programs are implemented because of the perception that teachers lack teaching skills. Many teachers believe that districts use such programs to teacher-proof the literacy curriculum. Even though all teachers in a school, district, or state are expected to use a core reading program for a portion of their literacy instruction, variation in quality of instruction still exists, demonstrating that such programs do not limit the quality of teaching. As might be expected, exemplary teachers refine such materials through the skill, flexibility, and ease with which they use their programs, resulting in outstanding student achievement (Pressley, 2006).

A final criticism, and one that we find troubling, is that the use of core reading programs results in unmotivated readers and writers. While core reading programs do select the literature for students and teachers, and choice is certainly important for motivating students (Gambrell, 1996), most of the text selections are quality children's literature published in an anthology format and selected to be engaging to students. Additionally, most programs are accompanied by a multitude of worksheets (the number of worksheets accompanying programs has grown over the years; some programs include more than a thousand for a single grade level). We believe that if teachers expect students to complete several of these every day, the result will be unmotivated students. So, yes, the core reading program can dampen student motivation, but as with other instructional events and materials, teachers can take steps to prevent that from happening.

## Literature-Based Literacy Curricula

Similar to core reading programs, literature-based literacy curricula are familiar in elementary classrooms. Smith (1979) and Goodman (1986) argued that teachers should move away from explicit instruction and toward more literature-rich engagement with authentic texts or children's books. Their writing led teachers to support what was known as "whole-language" literacy curricula. As whole-language instruction became more prevalent in classrooms, researchers investigated its merits (Pressley, 2006). A variety of strengths were noted, such as engaging children in literate behaviors as they learned to read and write (Morrow, 1991), the use of high-quality literature (Cochran-Smith, 1984), numerous writing activities, and growth of children's vocabulary (Elley, 1989).

Whole-language structures have been revised to reflect what is today considered balanced instruction, with typical whole-language emphases being balanced with skill-based instruction. Pearson, Raphael, Benson, and Madda (2007) discussed literacy instruction from the past and present and highlighted the importance of balance in a literacy curriculum. In their exploration of balance, they considered contextual and content factors. The former include authenticity, classroom discourse, teachers' roles, and curricular control. For authenticity, for example, academic concerns must be balanced with real-world concerns. Students need opportunities to engage in real tasks with real purposes, rather than only participating in school activities like completing comprehension worksheets (Florio-Ruane & Raphael, 2004). Pearson et al. considered such content areas as skill instruction, text genres, text difficulty, response to literature, subject matter emphasis, language arts, and reading instruction and identified balance within each of them. For skill instruction, teachers have to balance a predetermined curricular sequence with the needs of their students. They decide if all students need this skill instruction or if it would be better targeted to a small group of students who are still developing the particular skill.

Researchers like Worthy, Ivey, and Broaddus (2001) identified the importance of having books in classrooms that students want to read. They observed that in many intermediate classrooms there is a mismatch between what students want to read and what is available to them. They wrote, "Providing students with access to books that appeal to them is a crucial aspect of reading instruction." (p. 53) Worthy, Moorman, and Turner (1999) studied the preferences of elementary and middle school students. They discovered that students preferred scary books, comics, popular magazines, joke books, and informational books. Some of these were available to them in the classroom, but others, such as joke books or popular magazines, were not. So once again, balance comes into play—teachers support students by providing the books they believe are important as well as the books students prefer.

As with core reading programs, literature-based curricula are used for a number of reasons. Quality children's literature offers students opportunities to talk about books. Through this talk they build their own knowledge: knowledge about a variety of texts and genres, knowledge about words, and knowledge about themselves and the world (Tunnell & Jacobs, 2008). Moreover, exposure to multiple texts and the resulting discussion supports the development of literal, inferential, and critical comprehension (Anstey & Bull, 2006). And unlike the short, focused lessons within a core program, literature-based activities allow students to have prolonged experiences with text and writing that support deeper understanding of a theme or topic. Finally, literature-based curricula support student motivation by offering them a choice in book selection and writing activities (Pressley, Allington, Wharton-McDonald, Collins-Block, & Morrow, 2001).

It's no surprise that there has also been criticism of literature-based curricula. The central argument is that when an individual teacher develops his or her own curricula, there is no guarantee of consistency in literacy instruction among teachers in a grade level or from one year to the next. Some teachers may provide extensive time and practice for phonics skills but not for comprehension, while other teachers may privilege comprehension but not decoding. As a result, students may find some instruction to be redundant across grades, while other strategies or skills are never taught at all. That's not a great recipe for success. A second criticism is that teachers who work alone to provide instruction to students find it difficult to collaborate. Though using literature-based curricula does not necessarily result in teachers working as singletons, it can happen when each teacher develops his or her own literacy curricula. Similarly, it is more difficult for paraprofessionals and support teachers to work with teachers when curricula vary so widely. Further, as intervention blocks become more common in schools, determining what is best taught in such a block becomes more difficult if the students come from classes with different curricula. These issues can be overcome if attention is paid to them by teachers within and across grade levels—otherwise, they are potentially harmful to students' complete literacy development.

# Why It Is Important to Use Both

We believe that through the synchronized use of a core reading program and a literature-based approach, both you and your students benefit. Students benefit because they receive explicit, systematic, multilayered instruction in reading and writing. You benefit because you receive opportunities to shore up necessary foundational knowledge and skills for students as you creatively engage them in rich conversations and writing about reading experiences. More broadly, whole schools and districts benefit because they know that their students are receiving instruction that provides a foundation for independence and equips them to meet the appropriate standards.

Beyond our beliefs, there is a rich research base to support the use of both (Allington & Johnston, 2001; Ladson-Billings, 1994; Pressley et al., 2001; Taylor, Pearson, Clark, & Walpole, 2000). These studies found common characteristics of effective literacy learning, including the following:

- Explicit teaching of useful skills and strategies, targeted to the needs of students
- Differentiated instruction in which teachers provide appropriate materials to support students at various levels of ability in small-group or side-by-side teaching
- Small-group, whole-group, and side-by-side teaching, with whole-group instruction used for the smallest portion of the day
- Teacher-structured routines that hold students responsible for their work and behavior
- A focus on individual students' learning needs and strengths as determined through ongoing assessment by the teacher
- Integration of literacy skills and strategies throughout all curricular areas
- Managed choice of activities so that students have opportunities within topic areas to select books or writing topics or genres

- Rich literacy materials that include core reading materials, informational and narrative text, magazines, and Internet resources

These characteristics of exemplary literacy instruction are grounded in the use of both basal programs and literature-based instruction. Each of these characteristics supports the instruction described throughout this book. Further, Allington and Cunningham (2002) write that in the most effective classrooms, teachers used common texts for instruction some of the time, and students were not given a choice for all assignments. However, this more structured approach was balanced with the use of varied texts and choice in activities.

The goal for all literacy instruction should be students who are efficient at constructing meaning as they read text or creating meaning as they write text. Approaches that emphasize meaning only or skills only do not support this goal (Stahl & Miller, 2006). Meaning-only approaches limit students from developing decoding and other skills they need to get pleasure from children's literature. Skills-only approaches, with their focus on small aspects of reading or writing, likewise limit students' enjoyment of quality literature. Balancing the two approaches results in the strongest literacy instruction and learning. It moves beyond what Stahl (1998) labeled as the politicization of literacy instruction. He wrote:

> The politicization of recent years interferes with effective instruction because it hardens viewpoints and forces educators to adopt unreasonable tenets concerning instruction. One result of the movement is that teachers have a great many beliefs about reading instruction, some of which are tenable and some of which are not. As we approach the millennium, we need to step back, look at the evidence, and evaluate all our beliefs (p. 61).

This reflection on beliefs, critical in 1998, is even more so today. We worry that you may blame the politics of No Child Left Behind for the ways you currently instruct students. While No Child Left Behind has changed schools and classrooms, the intent of this law was never for students to sit through lectures followed by stacks of worksheets. If you feel trapped by this type of instruction, we are confident that you can find ways to move beyond it to engage students in the science and art of reading and writing. We hope this book provides the foundation for this thinking.

# Practical Matters

As you take up the challenge of using both approaches, you will be filled with questions that relate to the details. How can I find time to bring this instruction to my classroom? How should I go about this planning? What books should I use? This section responds to many of these practical concerns.

## When

While scheduling is never easy within an elementary school, it is necessary if teachers want to collaboratively use both approaches. It takes a leadership team to develop a schedule that works for all teachers and students. We have found that in schools where specific time blocks are set aside for literacy instruction, the literacy block and intervention blocks happen at different times for most grade levels. By setting schedules this way, paraprofessionals and support teachers can work with small groups of students during both of these times. The following chart (pages 21–22) shows one whole-school schedule for instruction that might be used as a model.

This schedule offers a place to begin as you consider how to schedule two literacy blocks and a writing block each day. Though this school does not have all of the literacy blocks at different times, teachers vary their whole-group and small-group times within the block. With this small change in student grouping, paraprofessionals and resource teachers can support differentiated small-group instruction. This school also provides daily literacy interventions to struggling students. By scheduling the literacy block next to the intervention block, teachers can extend the literacy block for students at grade level or above to an hour, rather than being limited to a half hour. Teachers also decided to focus on content-related lessons during the additional literacy block so that they would not have to plan for separate social studies and science blocks. On our last visit to this school, the intermediate teachers were feeling frustrated that they did not have sufficient time to delve more deeply into science and social studies. They were planning to eliminate morning and afternoon recesses to provide more time for students to engage in hands-on explorations during content-related instruction.

| WHOLE-SCHOOL INSTRUCTIONAL SCHEDULE | | | | | | | |
|---|---|---|---|---|---|---|---|
| TIMES | K | 1 | 2 | 3 | 4 | 5 | 6 |
| 9:00 | Intervention | Specials | Literacy Block | Literacy Block | Math | Literacy Block | Literacy Block |
| 9:15 | | | | | | | |
| 9:30 | Literacy Block | Literacy Block | | | | Intervention | |
| 9:45 | | | | | | | |
| 10:00 | Recess | | | | Intervention | Math | |
| 10:15 | Literacy Block | | | | | | |
| 10:30 | | | Recess | Recess | Literacy Block | | Recess |
| 10:45 | | | Intervention | Literacy Block | | | Math |
| 11:00 | | Recess and Lunch | | | Specials | Writing | |
| 11:15 | | | Literacy Block | Intervention | | | |
| 11:30 | | | | | Recess | | |
| 11:45 | Recess and Lunch | Math | Writing | Recess and Lunch | Writing | Recess and Lunch | Intervention |
| 12:00 | | | | | | | |
| 12:15 | | | | | | | Literacy Block |
| 12:30 | Specials | | Recess and Lunch | Writing | Recess and Lunch | Literacy Block | |
| 12:45 | | Recess | | | | | Recess and Lunch |
| 1:00 | Recess | Writing | | | | | |
| 1:15 | Math | | Specials | Specials | Computer | | |
| 1:30 | | | | | | | Writing |

| TIMES | K | 1 | 2 | 3 | 4 | 5 | 6 |
|---|---|---|---|---|---|---|---|
| 1:45 | Math | Intervention | Recess | Recess | Literacy Block | Literacy | Writing |
| 2:00 |  |  | Math | Math |  | Recess |  |
| 2:15 | Writing | Literacy Block |  |  |  | Specials | Specials |
| 2:30 |  |  |  |  |  |  |  |
| 2:45 |  |  |  |  |  |  |  |
| 3:00 |  |  |  |  |  |  |  |
| 3:05 | Dismissal |  |  |  |  |  |  |

*WHOLE-SCHOOL INSTRUCTIONAL SCHEDULE*

## How

### Standards

The how of using both begins with an exploration of national standards. The International Reading Association (IRA, www.reading.org) and the National Council of Teachers of English (NCTE, www.ncte.org) partnered to develop the following national literacy standards for students (International Reading Association and National Council of Teachers of English, 1996). Following are the standards from this document with brief descriptions.

1. Students read a wide range of print and nonprint texts to build an understanding of texts, of themselves, and of the cultures of the United States and the world; to acquire new information; to respond to the needs and demands of society and the workplace; and for personal fulfillment. Among these texts are fiction and nonfiction, classic and contemporary works.

2. Students read a wide range of literature from many periods in many genres to build an understanding of the many dimensions (e.g., philosophical, ethical, aesthetic) of human experience.

3. Students apply a wide range of strategies to comprehend, interpret, evaluate, and appreciate texts. They draw on their prior experience, their interactions with other readers and

writers, their knowledge of word meaning and of other texts, their word identification strategies, and their understanding of textual features (e.g., sound-letter correspondence, sentence structure, context, graphics).

4. Students adjust their use of spoken, written, and visual language (e.g., conventions, style, vocabulary) to communicate effectively with a variety of audiences and for different purposes.

5. Students employ a wide range of strategies as they write and use different writing process elements appropriately to communicate with different audiences for a variety of purposes.

6. Students apply knowledge of language structure, language conventions (e.g., spelling and punctuation), media techniques, figurative language, and genre to create, critique, and discuss print and nonprint texts.

7. Students conduct research on issues and interests by generating ideas and questions, and by posing problems. They gather, evaluate, and synthesize data from a variety of sources (e.g., print and nonprint texts, artifacts, people) to communicate their discoveries in ways that suit their purpose and audience.

8. Students use a variety of technological and information resources (e.g., libraries, databases, computer networks, video) to gather and synthesize information and to create and communicate knowledge.

9. Students develop an understanding of and respect for diversity in language use, patterns, and dialects across cultures, ethnic groups, geographic regions, and social roles.

10. Students whose first language is not English make use of their first language to develop competency in the English language arts and to develop understanding of content across the curriculum.

11. Students participate as knowledgeable, reflective, creative, and critical members of a variety of literacy communities.

12. Students use spoken, written, and visual language to accomplish their own purposes (e.g., for learning, enjoyment, persuasion, and the exchange of information).

While not all of these standards are addressed within this book, chapters 2, 3, and 4 incorporate many of them. We are sure that as you read these standards you noticed that they are similar to many of your district or state standards. It is also important for you to be familiar with these standards. By thoroughly understanding what content students at various grade levels are expected to master, you can make decisions about expanding the core literacy block. We recommend that grade-level teachers work together with these documents and their core reading program. You can decide where your program is sufficient and where it needs additional support to meet standards. This work can be used in following years—unless the state or district modifies standards or adopts new materials. Most states and districts include their standards for all content areas on their Web sites.

## Choices Within the Core Reading Program

Core reading programs offer a wealth of suggestions for instruction. They are organized by theme, with approximately four weeks of instruction targeted to the theme. During each week's cycle, a core text is the center of instruction, with supporting leveled texts for differentiated instruction. Most core reading programs also suggest related children's literature for additional instruction or for students' independent reading. As we peruse a teacher's edition for a theme within a grade level, we are often overwhelmed with all of the suggestions. Upon closer scrutiny, many of the suggestions, especially for independent work, can be put aside, as they do not offer sufficient reading or writing practice for students. For example, in one teacher's edition, students were encouraged to draw a crown in response to a text. Though students might enjoy the activity, it provided no opportunities for them to read or write.

To determine what should be targeted for instruction or practice from the core reading program, we suggest considering the following.

1. For direct instruction, focus on skills or strategies that are targeted for assessment. That's an indication that the skill or strategy is important for this grade level, and further instruction will build upon it.
2. Target instruction that is represented in district or state standards. These concepts have been determined to be important for students within a grade level.
3. Locate and use suggestions for reteaching or preteaching skills, strategies, or vocabulary for students requiring this additional instruction.
4. For independent work, incorporate only those suggestions that support students' reading and writing.

In many classrooms, we see teachers moving away from the discrete suggestions offered in the core program for independent student work. Instead, they use recurring activities for independent practice. Each day students reread text for decoding, comprehension, or fluency practice. They write in response to the text they just read, either with the whole class or in their small reading group. They may listen to the core text at a listening center, especially if they are struggling readers who need additional support. They might write in a journal. And finally, they might engage in word study, where they find and sort words representing a pattern that was highlighted in the core program.

Once you've determined the core program instruction, you are ready to consider expanding this curriculum with children's literature and reading and writing activities. We recommend that you target one core reading selection as the benchmark text for extended reading and writing. Though most selections in today's core reading programs are from children's literature (rather than texts written specifically for the program), some better lend themselves to extensions. As you make these decisions, we suggest you consider the following:

- Varying the genres that are selected throughout the year
- Selecting the work of authors or illustrators who have a significant number of books available. In this way, students can learn about an author or illustrator as they explore other elements of text
- Considering the text that best represents the theme
- Choosing text that easily supports other content extensions such as science or social studies

## Choices Within the Literature-Based Curricula

After you've chosen your core text, you're ready to gather other materials. There are many ways to go about this process. We have always begun close to home—by exploring our own personal library. We collect all of the books that might relate to the theme or to the benchmark text. Next, we ask our colleagues if they have any books relating to our theme, author, or text that they might lend us. Then, we might visit school or neighborhood libraries for books or materials. Bookstores might help as well, although once inside a bookstore, we are always prepared to buy more books than we intended. It is hard to walk away from a beautiful new children's book even if it has no connection to our theme. And today, we always visit the Internet to see what might be available to support our instruction.

Once you've assembled a rich array of materials, it is time for your imaginations to take off. When working with grade-level colleagues, we consider the important areas of literacy first. How can we use additional books to support comprehension, vocabulary, and fluency? We consider the importance of genre, illustrator or author studies, and writing. As with the core reading program, we envision more books and activities than are possible to use throughout a theme (about four weeks). We find this to be important, as various classes may value different activities or need different learning opportunities.

As we target specific books to use for additional instruction, we keep in mind how we might use them. For instance, Hartman and Hartman (1993) offer five possibilities to consider when making selections.

1. **Companion texts.** These books are meant to be read as a collection, with each book enriching the previous one.
2. **Complementary texts.** These books share a common topic or theme.
3. **Synoptic texts.** These books are variations of a single story, idea, or event.
4. **Disruptive texts.** These books offer conflicting perspectives on a topic, theme, event, or idea.
5. **Rereading texts.** These books are rich in complexity and are meant to be explored multiple times.

The first time we engaged in this planning process, it exhausted us. We generated multiple ideas, but then had to discard some of them because they did not support reading and writing development. As we repeated the process with other themes, we became more efficient. It was still tiring, but we accomplished the brainstorming in much less time. We knew that in future years we could use this thinking and planning and just revise as necessary.

## Assessment

Assessment permeates the use of both core reading programs and literature-based instruction. As students engage in reading and writing, teachers informally assess their development to plan future instruction. You may use the core reading assessments to guide this process. You may also use other forms of assessment, such as running records, fluency checks, or attitude surveys. You may provide rubrics for students so that they know what is expected of them on major assignments.

Teachers assess students during both instructional situations; assessment is not limited to the core reading portion of the day. Afflerbach (2007) notes that authentic assessment is grounded in the routine activities of students during reading and writing. Often it occurs during instruction: The teacher observes students' responses as she is teaching. For instance, a teacher may note that Bryan offered an inferential understanding of a text, marking the first time he moved beyond literal comprehension. The result of this informal assessment is to make appropriate decisions for instruction and grouping of students throughout all literacy instruction.

Many teachers use portfolios, for which both teachers and students select work (Barone & Taylor, 2007). Portfolios help teachers and students take the long view of literacy development.

Considering one piece of work on one day offers a one-dimensional view of a student. By collecting samples of their work over a whole academic year, intermediate students have a record of their growth. With teacher support, they can determine both their strengths and the areas that still need attention.

Now, as we near the end of this first chapter, it is time for you to uncross those arms and begin. The process of using both may not be easy, but it is exhilarating. Watching students develop the foundation for reading and writing as they engage in rewarding literature-rich activities is invigorating and provides you with the energy to continue with this process. Rather than letting a set of materials be limiting, this process opens up all materials—core programs, literature, software, newspapers, magazines, lists—for instruction.

Using both results in readers and writers who go beyond just deciphering the print on a page. They bring new levels of understanding to the words on the page as they make connections, explore new words, participate in critical discussions, and build bridges between what they experience and what is possible.

The next three chapters share potential ways to integrate the core reading program and literature-based curricula. We have selected benchmark texts from several core reading programs and envisioned multiple ways to engage students in literature-rich reading and writing. We know you're probably thinking, "Well, all of these suggestions can only work with a specific program, so they don't pertain to me." Not so. Most of the suggestions offered are not limited to one program, one theme, or one selection. They can be used within multiple extensions of any program or theme. We believe these examples will help you support your students to further develop as readers and writers, for we know that the most important factor in student learning is the quality of teaching provided to them (Haycock, 1998; Marzano, 2003).

# CHAPTER 2

# *F*ourth-Grade Possibilities

*The love of reading cannot be taught generally; it depends on contact with specific titles, certain subjects, and particular authors. To catch students, an enormously wide variety of books of different formats and levels of difficulty need to be available in the elementary classroom.* —Michael Tunnell and James Jacobs (2008)

As promised, this chapter contains an overview of a 90-minute literacy block that uses a core reading program. We targeted Theme One, This Land Is Your Land, from the Scott Foresman core reading series (2007), chose a benchmark text from this theme, and wrote about ways we would instruct students with the core program. Then we reflected and came up with a multitude of ideas that could be used in a second literacy block with any core program. You may notice that we became a bit excited about the possibilities and generated many more activities than any one teacher would want to do with students. However, we decided to list them all to give you plenty of choices when you're selecting what best fits a group of students and/or particular theme.

## The Core Reading Program

The theme, This Land Is Your Land, incorporates nine major text selections and Internet sources. The texts are *Because of Winn-Dixie* by Kate DiCamillo; *Fast Facts: Black Bears* by Kathy Kranking; *Lewis and Clark and Me* by Laurie Myers; *They Traveled With Lewis and Clark* by Elizabeth Massie; *Grandfather's Journey* by Allen Say; *The Horned Toad Prince* by Jackie Hopkins; *Horned Lizards and Harvesting Ants* by John Brown; *Letters Home From Our National Parks: Yosemite* by Lisa Halvorsen; and *This Land Is Your Land* by Woody Guthrie. The selections are rich in genre—there is informational text, poetry, realistic fiction, historical fantasy, historical fiction, modern fairy tales, and narrative nonfiction. *A Look at Two Lands* contains an online-text component. The core reading program authors also selected texts that target disciplinary areas such as social studies and science. It was no easy task to select just one benchmark text from this theme, although we finally decided upon *Letters Home From Our National Parks: Yosemite*. We believe that narrative nonfiction is a more unusual genre for students to explore and offers numerous possibilities for extension. You might decide on any one of these, as each could stand as a benchmark text. No decision is necessarily better than another; the final test is whether the selection and the activities surrounding it result in increased student learning and engagement.

*Letters Home From Our National Parks: Yosemite* begins with a collage of items posted on a photo of Yosemite. The items include binoculars, letters, a visitor's guide, a flower, and a compass. The initial illustration offers an opportunity for rich discussion, as do similar illustrations throughout the book. There is also a question posed—Why do so many people travel to Yosemite National Park?—and a description of the genre, narrative nonfiction. Each page shares a portion of a journey to the park, and this organization helps keep key elements discrete. The first page, a description of a child's arrival in San Francisco, shares a few facts  about Yosemite. The next page, headed with the word "Topography," describes the park, mountains, and early settlers, who called Yosemite "Ahwahnee." The next page, "Badger Pass," shares photos and a map of Yosemite. The visitor shares his or her entry to the park at Badger Pass. Following is a page that describes the Yosemite Valley and Bridal Veil Falls. The next pages move away from geography and share information about the giant sequoias and wildlife. The book then focuses on interesting parts of the park, such as Glacier Point, El Capitan, Yosemite Falls, Mt. Lyell, and Tioga Pass, and ends with descriptions of these areas.

This selection and the leveled texts associated with it come with numerous teaching and learning expectations.

**Comprehension**

- Students are to focus on the main idea in this selection. They use details to generate this main idea.
- After reading, students are to share what they know about the author.

- Students are asked to respond to the content the author used to get at critical analysis (Why do you think she included the names of several giant sequoias?)
- Students should compare and contrast Yosemite in the past with today.
- Students are to use preview and prediction to discover the kinds of information in this selection.
- Students are to explore fact and opinion within the selection.

**Word Knowledge**

Vocabulary
- Students are to become familiar with these words (*glacier, impressive, naturalist, preserve, species, slopes, wilderness, altitudes, formations,* and *reservoir*).

Phonics/Decoding
- Students are to practice words with long *u*.

Word Structure
- Students are to consider suffixes and their connections to meaning (*-ist* and *-ive*). The words they use are *naturalist* and *impressive*.

**Fluency**

- Students are to reread the text and/or listen to it on CD and follow along with the text.
- Teachers are expected to model phrasing with students imitating.
- Students are to echo-read at various points throughout the text.
- Students are to read with a partner.

**Writing to Learn**

- Students are to write notes about what they know about national parks in general and about any specific park before reading.
- Students are to write new information as they discover it in reading.
- Students are to write about why the author used photos and letters to illustrate the text.
- Students are expected to use graphic organizers to support comprehension. They use a web with supporting details.
- Students are to write daily summaries of the text.
- Students are to write connections across the texts (core selection and leveled texts).

**Writing**

- Students learn about clauses and complex sentences.

- Students practice writing a narrative for a test.
- Students write a postcard.
- Students participate in an Internet inquiry activity where they explore the unique qualities of the West.

This single selection generated many specific goals for learning. Some, like the long-vowel work, are review practice. Multiple comprehension activities help students understand literally, inferentially, and critically. As well, the publisher has offered numerous ways for students to engage in writing to extend comprehension of this text.

Leveled texts support the above activities as well as strategies that all students are expected to know and use, such as understanding the big ideas in these selections. So, within this program are opportunities for whole-class learning and differentiated small-group practice, and extension of the strategies and skills. At each level, there are numerous activities that students might engage in. It's always best to target the most important strategies and skills and teach these to students, rather than superficially teaching all the skills and strategies offered for instruction. Similarly, if you use the practice worksheets, you need to select the most appropriate ones for your students, as the program offers more than any one child should be expected to complete. You may want to avoid work sheets entirely, instead offering students opportunities to read and write in more authentic ways for independent practice.

# The Extended Literacy Curriculum

We have chosen two complementary foci for extending the benchmark selection. The first extension offers students multiple opportunities to learn about U.S. national parks. Because these parks are protected wilderness areas, for the second, we selected novels with characters living in rugged areas outside of cities. As students learn about the details of the parks, they also share adventures of characters exploring similar areas. We provide ways for students to create journals and narrative writing of their own about adventures in the wilderness.

## Reading Connections

### Fiction

There are many books that focus on children surviving in the wild. Taboada, Guthrie, and McRae (2008) have found that adventure stories are of high interest to intermediate students and they are easily engaged in reading and chatting about them. We list a few of these books and provide brief summaries. You may want to use several of these titles for small-group or book club reading. Having multiple titles available for students gives them a range of options within the focus you have chosen. Students have opportunities to talk about the book they are reading with other students who are reading the same text, and they can have whole-class discussions comparing plots, settings, or characters among the books.

*Hatchet* (Paulsen, 2006). This Newbery Honor book may be familiar to many teachers. Brian Robeson is on his way to visit his father in the Canadian north country. The bush pilot he is flying with has a heart attack, so Brian is left in a plane with no pilot or other passengers. The plane crashes and Brian discovers that he must survive in the wild. He learns how to build a fire, to hunt, and to protect himself against the elements and animals. He also relies on information that he heard his parents or teachers say and on information from films to help him survive.

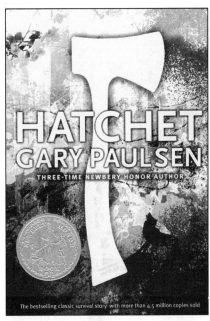

*Julie of the Wolves* (George, 1972). *Julie of the Wolves* is another Newbery award winner. In addition to her English name, the title character is also known as Miyax, her name in Eskimo. Forced into a marriage as a young girl, Julie leaves her husband and attempts to find her pen pal in San Francisco. She returns to Alaska and learns to live in the Alaskan wilderness with wolves that help her. Julie, like several characters, becomes a careful observer of animal behavior so that she can coexist with them.

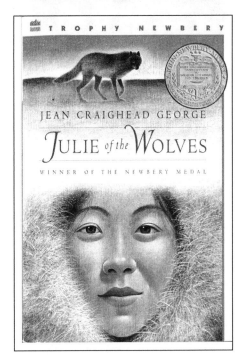

*My Side of the Mountain* (George, 1988). Sam Gribley leaves home to live in the Catskill Mountains. He learns to survive, and as he settles in the wild, friends and family visit. Unlike the other stories, Sam lives in the mountains because he has chosen to do so (and his parents have allowed him to), rather than because of an accident or because he had run away or was trying to get to another place. There are many similarities between this book and *Hatchet*; both boys learn to make a shelter and then to make fire, fish, and hunt for survival.

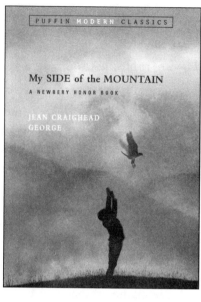

*Kidnapped: Book Three: The Rescue* (Korman, 2006).

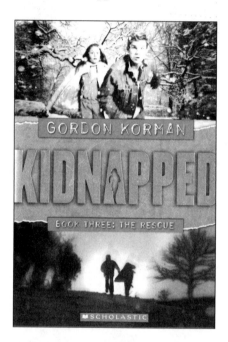

The author has written several adventure stories for adolescents. This book is the third in a trilogy about the Falconer family. Meg, Aiden Falconer's sister, was kidnapped in earlier episodes. In this book, she escapes and has to survive in the mountains and find safety in a snowstorm. She finds a shelter and must learn to build a fire. During her encounter with a bear and other challenges, she relies on information she remembers from science lessons. This present-day survival tale includes phones and the Internet.

*The Fear Place* (Naylor, 1996). This story centers

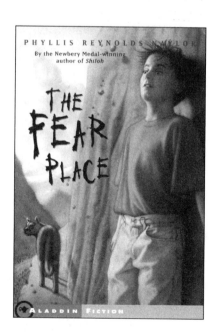

on Doug Grillo's vacation in Colorado. He has a fight with his brother, who then leaves the family and goes off on his own. While trying to find him, Doug is scared as he walks along narrow ledges. A cougar he meets along the way helps him find his brother.

This book has several things in common with the others. The first is the theme of a child alone, who must conquer fears as he maneuvers and survives in the wild. The second is that he often finds help through a wild animal, in this case a cougar. Third, he often thinks about things his parents or others have said or recalls information from books to solve dilemmas. Here, Doug remembers his mother telling him to be cautious as he negotiates the ledge. Finally, the child is successful at surviving in the wild.

These themes could certainly be compared as students read several wilderness tales. Students will learn about the character's inner strength to survive, but perhaps most important to intermediate boys, the books are filled with action.

## Nonfiction

We begin the exploration of national parks by revisiting the benchmark selection, *Letters Home From Our National Parks: Yosemite* (Halvorsen, 2000). We encourage you to use this text, or texts like it, as a model for building a chart that supports students as they engage in learning the details of individual parks and making connections across parks. The chart might look something like the one in Figure 2.1. Later, in writing extensions, students are asked to use the geography of a specific park to build an adventure story.

When you investigate a new park, add it to the chart or create a new one. This information provides opportunities for further investigations and serves as a source of details about the parks. For instance, if students decide that they want to know more about mule deer or sequoias, they can use this baseline data for their inquiries.

We found one book, *M Is for Majestic* (Domeniconi, 2007), that provides interesting tidbits of information about all of the parks. It is arranged alphabetically but its content is quite sophisticated. It begins with a map of the U.S. and the locations of all the national parks (there are more than 50). Though the majority of the parks are in the West, with California and Alaska having the most, there are eight in the Midwest and East. Each page shares information about specific national parks. Each page has a variety of ways to share

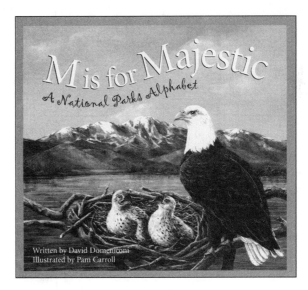

information. The main text is written as a poem, with text boxes on each side that provide information about the parks. Finally, there are painted illustrations with photos, similar to postcards, attached to each illustration. The illustration style is similar to Halvorsen's in *Letters Home From Our National Parks: Yosemite*. The book begins with the *A*'s—Acadia National Park

### Figure 2.1: YOSEMITE PARK TEXT SUPPORT CHART

| IMPORTANT DATES | TOPOGRAPHY | FEATURES | WILDLIFE | PLANT LIFE |
|---|---|---|---|---|
| Lincoln, 1864: Yosemite Grant | In Sierra Nevada mountains | Badger Pass—ski place | Black bear—300 to 500 in the park | Giant Sequoias can grow to over 300 feet tall and can live more than 3,000 years |
| John Muir fought to make it a park | 15.5 million acres | Yosemite Valley—most heavily visited part of park | Mule deer—have long ears like mules | Grizzly Sequoia is the oldest in park |
| Became a national park on October 1, 1890 | Native Americans were first people to live in park | Bridal Veil Falls is 620 feet high (equivalent to a 62-story building) | 240 species of birds including peregrine falcons | |
| 3.5 million people visit park each year | Ahwahnee—place of Gaping Mouth | Glacier Point is 3,200 feet above the valley | | |
| | | El Capitan—biggest single block of granite on earth | | |
| | | Yosemite Falls—highest waterfall in U.S. | | |

in Maine, the National Park of American Samoa, and Arches National Park in Utah.

Although you can share this book with the whole class, students will also want to spend time investigating the illustrations and details presented in the text. There isn't extensive information about any one park, but students get an understanding about the number and variety of parks in the U.S. and the unique aspects of each one.

*National Parks* (Petersen, 2001) is organized as a simple informational chapter book. There is a table of contents, glossary, and index, and its reading level makes it accessible to most fourth graders. This book provides a general overview of national parks around the world. It notes that Yellowstone, created in 1872, was the

## MORE NATIONAL PARKS TITLES FROM CHILDREN'S PRESS

*Acadia National Park* by Wende Fazio

*Arches National Park* by David Petersen

*Bryce Canyon National Park* by David Petersen

*Chaco Culture National Park* by David Petersen

*Death Valley National Park* by David Petersen

*Denali National Park and Preserve* by David Petersen

*Everglades National Park* by Wende Fazio

*Grand Canyon National Park* by David Petersen

*Great Sand Dunes National Park* by David Petersen

*Haleakala National Park* by David Petersen

*Hawaii Volcanoes National Park* by Sharlene Nelson & Ted Nelson

*Isle Royale National Park* by Joan Kalbacken

*Mount Rainier National Park* by Sharlene Nelson & Ted Nelson

*Mount St. Helens National Volcanic Monument* by Sharlene Nelson & Ted Nelson

*Olympic National Park* by Sharlene Nelson & Ted Nelson

*Petrified Forest National Park* by David Petersen

*Saguaro National Park* by David Petersen

*Yellowstone National Park* by David Petersen

Each of these books offers details about a particular national park. Within each book are additional resources to support student inquiry. For instance, *Acadia National Park* lists books about Maine and the seacoast. Many of the books also point to corresponding Web sites, such as the one for Acadia National Park (www.nps.gov/acad) and for the National Park Service (www.nps.gov). Each park also has its own Web site on nps.gov, with photos and interesting information.

first true national park, and that there are now more than 1,200 worldwide. The author helps readers understand the differences between national parks and monuments. National parks have combinations of features such as scenery, wildlife, and historical sites, while national monuments have one main feature. This book is one in a large series, by Petersen and other authors, investigating national parks.

## Writing Connections

We suggest two multilayered writing connections as extensions for this theme: creating a journal and writing an adventure story. For both exercises, students select one national park as the setting. First, they revisit the chart with information about a particular park. If there is a book targeting that particular park, they reread it for additional details. Finally, students visit the park's Web site for even more details. Once they have satisfied they understand the details about the national park chosen, they might do a quick sketch that captures the important features of the park or choose a photo from the Internet. For the second extension, students may want to target one location from the first sketch or photo as the setting for their survival story.

### Writing Extension 1: A Journal of Survival

In this extension, students create journals as they explore a national park. We found two useful models for this writing extension. In the My America series, children share their diaries of moving west. Two examples from the series are *A Perfect Place: Joshua's Oregon Trail Diary* (Hermes, 2002) and *For This*

*Land: Meg's Prairie Diary* (McMullan, 2003). First, read the books to students to serve as a model for their writing. Then, have students revisit their selected national park, and, as though they were explorers, create diaries from the time they enter the park until they leave. In their journals, students should include the important features of the park, as well as the adventures they have there. This writing is more structured through explicit teacher directions and could serve as a foundation for the greater challenge of writing an adventure story.

## Writing Extension 2: An Adventure Story

In this extension, students create adventure stories similar to those they read. They choose a particular place in their national park as the setting for their story. Then they decide on a character. They may want to create a chart with information about the character's personality (see Figure 2.2). They can use this information as they craft their stories. Writing an adventure story is a complex undertaking—such charts provide support for students when writing becomes difficult.

Before they start their first draft, you may want them to plot their stories by brainstorming and listing key events that will occur. With all the prewriting in place, they should be excited and prepared to craft their own adventure stories. Several days should be allotted for the actual writing. Students write first drafts, consult with one another and you for revision, revise, and then move to a final draft. Once all of the stories are complete, students can share them with one another and perhaps with their parents in a special school event. These stories might be compiled into an anthology of adventure stories for further reading.

Both of these writing extensions require time. In each, students are layering their knowledge of parks, characters, and adventures within a particular genre. By having students create journals first, much of the thinking for the more complicated adventure story has already happened. Reading at least one adventure story, either from the books mentioned in the journal extension or from one you and your students have discovered, should also help prepare them for writing adventure stories of their own.

### Figure 2.2: INFORMATION ABOUT CALLIE

| Callie | She is in fourth grade in Wyoming. |
|---|---|
| | She is going on a field trip with her class to Teton National Park. |
| | She loves animals. She even has her own horse that she trains. |
| | She likes adventures. |
| | She is smart in school and likes to read. |

## Author/Illustrator Study

In addition to *Letters Home From Our National Parks: Yosemite*, Lisa Halvorsen has written many other books in the form of letters home that would serve well as the basis for an author study. You might begin with her other books about national parks (Grand Canyon and Zion) and then move to her books about countries. Students may wonder how she chose the countries and what they can learn about these countries from her books. Although the author does not have a Web site, we understand that she is very interested in travel and conducts tours. They may also wonder why she always uses the same organizing topic (letters home) and format. This is a much tougher question, and students need to form their own reasons, with support from her books, to answer it.

## Extension of the Core Reading Program Theme

By targeting the country's national parks, we've incorporated the theme, This Land Is Your Land, into all of our extension activities. Through this focus, students learn about the wilderness areas of the United States that have been protected for their enjoyment. For children who live in cities, this may be the first time they have learned about these protected areas.

## Vocabulary Extensions

When we taught this theme, our students collected interesting words as they read about national parks, and worked on and read survival stories and journals. Rather than our deciding which words should be studied, we placed students in charge. We asked a small group of fourth graders to engage in this process with *My Side of the Mountain*. They chose the following words and recorded them on sticky notes as they read: *hemlock*, *whittled*, *primitive*, *gorge*, and *barometer*.

### SEVEN TITLES FROM LISA HALVORSEN

*Letters Home From Italy*

*Letters Home From Peru*

*Letters Home From Turkey*

*Letters Home From Our National Parks: Grand Canyon*

*Letters Home From Our National Parks: Yosemite*

*Letters Home From Our National Parks: Zion*

*Letters Home From Zimbabwe*

There may have been other words these students didn't recognize or had trouble with, but they selected only these five.

Students then used the Longman Online Dictionary (www.ldoceonline.com) to find definitions of these words. (We selected this dictionary because it has student-friendly definitions.) They discovered that *hemlock* is a very poisonous plant; *to whittle* means to shape a piece of wood by cutting off small pieces with a knife; *primitive* means something that is very simple and does not have the extra modern parts that would make it faster, better, or more comfortable; a *gorge* is a deep narrow valley with steep sides; and a *barometer* is an instrument that measures changes in the air pressure, which can be used to forecast changes in the weather and determine height above sea level. They were satisfied with all of the definitions except for *hemlock*. They didn't think it had anything to do with poison when they read it in their book so they checked out different kinds of trees. They used Google as a search engine and discovered that *hemlock* is also a large, evergreen tree (www.arborday.org).

Students might collect these words in a booklet or personal dictionary to which they can add words throughout the year. Students told us that they loved picking out their own words to learn, rather than always having the words selected by their teachers.

Our second vocabulary activity was to find words related to survival in the wilderness and list them on a class chart. Each student had a bookmark with "Survival Words" written at the top. As they read the books about national parks and the survival stories, they jotted down words and noted the book titles and page numbers where they were found. At right is an example of one student's bookmark.

Once students had completed one or two bookmarks, they worked with a partner. The partners collapsed their words into one set and determined categories they could use to sort them. Categories might include weather words or sense words. After sorting their lists into categories, the partners joined with another partnership and formed a group of four. This group completed the same process. Finally, the whole class completed a master sort of survival words that was placed on a chart for students to refer to and add to. Students were able to refer to the chart as a resource as they wrote their own survival stories.

> **Survival Words**
>
> Thundering waterfalls
> (p. 27, Nat'l Parks)
>
> Zero visibility
> (p. 34, Kidnapped)
>
> Kindling
> (p. 38, Kidnapped)

## Ties to Content Areas Such as Social Studies and Science

The theme, This Land Is Your Land, offers numerous opportunities for students to make connections to social studies or science. Social studies teachers might study John Muir, one of the most famous U.S. naturalists. As he traveled in the West, he wrote about its natural beauty. Because of the role his writing played in their formation, Muir is considered to be the father of our national parks. He also helped found the Sierra Club. There is much information about John Muir on the Sierra Club Web site. Students may be interested to learn that, through the Sierra Club, his work still influences many legal cases related to protection of the environment. The Sierra Club recently sued the University of Wisconsin, where John Muir studied, because the school purchased a coal-fired power plant that resulted in pollution that violated the Clean Air Act. See the chart below for Web sites with information about John Muir.

Connections to science are numerous as well, as each park is filled with animals, plants, and trees. To begin science investigations, teachers might share *"Hey Ranger!" Kids Ask Questions About Yellowstone National Park* (Justesen, 2006). The book is organized around questions from young visitors to the park. The first is "Where did Yellowstone come from?" Other questions focus on important physical elements of Yellowstone: "Why can't we swim in the hot springs?" and "Why are the

### WEB SITES WITH INFORMATION ABOUT JOHN MUIR

| | |
|---|---|
| www.nps.gov/jomu | This site is sponsored by the U.S. National Park Service. It shares photos of Muir and of his home. |
| www.ecotopia.org | This site discusses John Muir as part of the Ecology Hall of Fame. It includes a biography, bibliography, and Web links. |
| www.myhero.com | This site includes a biography of Muir as one of Earth's keepers. |
| www.pcta.org | This site shares information about the John Muir Trail in Yosemite Valley. |
| www.sierraclub.org | This site provides a fascinating overview of the ways in which John Muir's life work has influenced the Sierra Club. |

hot springs, like Mammoth, drying up?"
Still others focus on the wildlife in the park:
"How old do deer have to be before they
turn into elk?" or "Why did you bring
wolves to the park? Won't they mess everything up?" The questions in this book
model the kinds of questions we envision
students posing as they read. While you
may want students to do extensive reports
about the landscape or elements in a park
such as plants and trees, or the animals, we

believe students will enjoy finding answers to a single question. The questions and answers could
then be compiled into a class book that students can use as a resource for other investigations.

Marcus, a fourth grader, decided to research coyotes. He wanted to know how coyotes survive in the
wild. We observed as he investigated. He found a
book and Internet sources for information to answer
his question. He began with *Bugling Elk and Sleeping
Grizzlies* (Craighead, 2004). He found out that wolves
prey on coyotes, especially young ones. He then went
to the Internet. He visited www.desertusa.com, where
he learned about the coyote and viewed film clips of
coyotes in the wild. He was disappointed, though, as
he did not learn about wolves. He then went to
http://kids.nationalgeographic.com/Animals/
CreatureFeature/Coyote, which also listed wolves as
a predator of coyotes. At this site, he watched a

video of coyote pups. Even though Marcus was only trying to answer one question about coyotes,
he left this investigation knowing quite a bit about them.

## Visual Literacy Extensions and Technology Connections

There are visual literacy opportunities throughout this exploration of national parks. In
Halvorsen's work, there is an interesting mix of visual elements on each page. The background

typically consists of a large photo with smaller photos layered on top of it. Text is always in a text box and is organized to resemble a PowerPoint slide. You may encourage students to use this format to make their own PowerPoint presentations to share information about their selected Parks. Figure 2.3 shows a slide from a student's PowerPoint presentation.

**Figure 2.3: POWERPOINT SLIDE**

Teton Park
These are mountains in the park. If you were going to the park, you would need a tent to sleep in and a backpack for your stuff.

Many of the books about parks use photos to provide images of the park and its wildlife. Students can also visit Web sites about the parks and explore additional images. We wondered what thoughts students would learn about parks through an exploration of photos. Students might begin with a book and just consider the photos. We found that Web sites offered more opportunities to explore photos. At www.shannontech.com, we found images of Grand Teton National Park organized by categories such as park features, trees, roads, sunsets, and birds. To model thinking about the images, teachers might project an image of the park and ask students to describe it as an artist would. Then they can describe the same photo as a park ranger, then as a naturalist. Finally, they could compare their descriptions from various points of view. Thinking as visual artists allows students to expand their conceptions of the geography of a park beyond the written word.

## Connections to Technology

Not surprisingly, there are numerous ways to connect an exploration of national parks to technology. We envision students creating PowerPoint presentations, as shared in the previous section. This exploration also allows students to visit numerous Web sites connected to parks (see chart, page 45).

## U.S. NATIONAL PARKS

| www.nps.gov | All of the U.S. national parks can be found here. |
|---|---|
| www.areaParks.com | This site offers information about all U.S. national parks. |
| www.yosemitePark.com | This site offers information about Yosemite. There is a similar site for each park. |
| http://library.thinkquest.org/3627 | This site shows 15 parks in the U.S. and is developed by kids for kids. |
| http://kids.nationalgeographic.com | This site offers information about the parks and animals. |
| www.scholastic.com | When you search "national parks," this site offers articles and activities pertinent to national parks. |

All of these sites will help students better understand national parks. Teachers can use the sites to generate additional ideas or activities for students.

# Connections to Fourth-Grade Literacy Standards

In Chapter 1, we shared the national standards formulated by the International Reading Association and the National Council of Teachers of English. For the instruction shared in this chapter, the following national standards (9 of 12) have been addressed: standards 1, 3, 4, 5, 6, 7, 8, 11, and 12. You can feel confident that the instruction shared here targets these national standards.

National standards are important, but we know that you are more closely connected to your state standards, since student assessments are based on them. For fourth grade, we reviewed Michigan's language arts standards (www.michigan.gov/documents/ELAGLCE_140483_7.pdf), which are separated into four divisions: reading, writing, speaking, and listening and viewing.

In reading, fourth graders are expected to know about words and their structure, read fluently, understand the meaning of words, and be able to use a thesaurus and dictionary. The reading standards are further divided between narrative and informational text.

**In narrative text students will:**

- describe the shared human experience depicted in classic, multicultural, and contemporary literature recognized for quality and literary merit.
- identify and describe the structure, elements, and purpose of a variety of narrative genres, including poetry, myths, legends, fantasy, and adventure.
- analyze characters' thoughts and motivation through dialogue, various character roles, and functions including hero, anti-hero, or narrator; know first-person point of view and identify conflict and resolution.
- explain how authors use literary devices, including flash-forward and flashback to depict time, setting, conflicts, and resolutions to enhance the plot and create suspense.

**In informational text students will:**

- identify and describe the structure, elements, features, and purpose of a variety of informational genre, including autobiography/biography, personal essay, almanac, and newspaper.
- identify and describe informational text patterns, including compare/contrast, cause/effect, and problem/solution.
- explain how authors use text features, including appendices, headings, subheadings, marginal notes, keys and legends, figures, and bibliographies, to enhance the understanding of key and supporting ideas (Michigan Department of Education, 2006).

The majority of these expectations are achieved through the core program and additional literacy activities that have been described.

The reading standards are further broken down into standards for comprehension, metacognition, critical standards, and reading attitude. Within the comprehension standards, students are expected to connect personal knowledge and experiences to oral and written response, to build relationships among characters and themes, and to apply knowledge to social studies and science. These specific areas have been well supported in the instruction provided. One additional note: You could ask students to build rubrics for any of the investigations we describe. We believe student attitude is addressed throughout this exploration, as there are numerous opportunities for them to make their own decisions about what they are going to read and write.

The next major area in the fourth-grade standards is writing. The broad expectations are that students be able to write in various genres. One further expectation is that students use personal style in their writing, which includes voice, among other qualities. We believe the writing activities shared here address these standards in an exemplary way—students have multiple opportunities to write for learning and to create a journal or adventure story. The journals provide a perfect opportunity for students to use voice in their writing.

The next two major areas are speaking and listening. There are many opportunities throughout for students to listen to their teacher and other students as they explore their park, details for their story, and personal questions. The PowerPoint presentations also provide students with opportunities to share using authentic tools, engaging them in listening and responding.

Throughout this chapter we have shared thought-provoking ways to engage students in reading and writing activities. The core program and literature-rich activities coexist and support one another—each working together to create a more complete reading and writing experience for students.

# CHAPTER 3

# *F*ifth-Grade Possibilities

*To me the most humbling part of observing accomplished teachers is seeing the sub-tle ways in which they build emotionally and relationally healthy learning com-munities—intellectual environments that produce not mere technical competence, but caring, secure, actively literate human beings. Observing these teachers accomplish both goals convinced me that the two achievements are not completely at odds.*

—Peter Johnston (2004)

We chose this quote because it emphasizes blending explicit instruction with creating a literate environment. In Chapter 1 we discussed the importance of looking to your core program as a base from which to build this environment. The classroom Johnston describes is not one at the margins of a core program but one in which an exemplary teacher with knowledge of the reading process and children's literature *and* the ability to move beyond the core program creates an envi-ronment in which children are engaged in authentic, meaningful literate practices. Throughout this chapter we hope to inspire you to create classrooms full of engagement and insight, where children receive the explicit instruction they need to become literate human beings. This chapter also focuses on the importance of talk in the classroom—and how to move away from the recom-mended language in the core program, which talks *at* children, and toward a more discussion-ori-ented way of talking *with* children. We want to empower children and help teachers create learn-ing environments that meet all students' needs.

To explore fifth-grade possibilities, we chose the Macmillan/McGraw-Hill core reading pro-gram (2007) and selected Theme One, Challenges. This is a common theme in children's litera-ture. Many biographies and works of realistic fiction, expository writing, and historical fiction are framed around a challenge the protagonist must overcome. This theme creates many opportuni-ties to explore exciting titles across genres and to engage students in meaningful extension activi-ties that enhance their understanding of literature.

# The Core Reading Program

The Challenges theme focuses on five different genres: realistic fiction, tall tales, magazines, expository writing, and fantasy. Each of the text selections—*Miss Alaineus* by Debra Frasier; *Davy Crockett Saves the World* by Rosalyn Schanzer; *Forests of the World* by the editors of *Time for Kids*; *Ultimate Field Trip 5: Blasting Off to Space Academy* by Susan Goodman; and *Pipiolo and the Roof Top Dogs* by Brian Meunier—approaches the theme in a different way.

The benchmark text we chose for this theme was *Miss Alaineus: A Vocabulary Disaster*, a realistic fiction selection. The story is about Sage, a little girl who is at home sick and tries to find out what assignments she missed in school. She calls a friend, but the friend is in a rush and tells her the vocabulary list too quickly over the phone. Sage misunderstands the last word on the list, *miscellaneous*, which leads to all sorts of events that happen to her throughout the rest of the story.

When she returns to school, her misunderstanding becomes obvious to her classmates, who laugh at her when she presents her words in front of the class. Sage is challenged to overcome her humiliation and to think of a way to solve her problem. With the help of her mother, she comes up with an idea to turn the mistake into a triumph. Frasier humorously infuses vocabulary words throughout the story. *Miss Alaineus* is a great way for students to engage in conversations about the academic and social challenges they face every day in school. The core reading program addresses many specific skills and strategies through this text. The list that follows describe the core reading program's expectations for student engagement with this text.

### Oral Language—Listening, Speaking, and Viewing

- Students are asked to focus on the question *What challenges, responsibilities and emotions are involved in contests?*
- Students build background knowledge by talking about contests.
- Teacher reads aloud the story *La Bamba* to access prior knowledge.
- Students listen to the teacher read aloud and pay attention to fluency, phrasing, expression, and tone of voice.

- Students expand vocabulary by locating words in the read-aloud that connect to the theme.

## Word Knowledge
### Vocabulary
- Students learn to read words in context.
- Students focus on these words: *soggy, strands, capable, categories, gigantic, credit,* and *luminous.*
- Students look at content vocabulary: *competition, orally,* and *eliminate.*

### Phonics/Decoding
- Students work with words that contain short vowels and attend to the CVC and CVCC patterns.
- Students study the words *luck, lock, sack, bend, tick, sung, rent, bath, ramp,* and *rust* and identify the short vowel pattern.

### Spelling
- Students focus on short vowel patterns with words such as *just, cot, stump, tough, laugh, guess, batch, rough, gush,* etc.
- Students complete a variety of word sorts with these words and sort by short vowel sounds.

## Comprehension
- Students learn the skill of identifying character and plot and then analyze the various features and how they impact the story.
- Students discuss the importance of setting in the text.
- Students connect and compare the story to the read-aloud and the overall theme of challenges.

## Writing
- Students write in response to daily prompts about entering a contest, proposing a contest, and talents that would help them win a contest.
- Students engage in the writing process to draft, revise, proofread, and publish a personal narrative.

### Grammar
- Students focus on the structure of a sentence.
- Students identify complete and incomplete sentences.

- Students focus on commands and exclamations.
- Students learn about the mechanics and usage of sentences as they punctuate sentences properly.

In addition, this core program has numerous class-management suggestions. It recommends small, differentiated instruction groups with leveled readers and provides an "independent learning contract" for students to use to guide them in their independent work. The contract includes checklists for independent reading, writing, social studies, technology, word study, science, leveled readers, and independent practice with work sheets. For each suggestion mentioned above there are numerous recommendations for independent workstations. We would like you to carefully consider—or rather, reconsider—what students are doing in independent centers or workstations. Be sure that your centers are worthy of the time students spend in them. In other words, make sure that what your students are doing in centers is as valuable as reading quietly for 40 minutes.

We also recommend that you not build a center around a writing project unless you have had a chance to provide explicit instruction within a writing workshop setting. It's fine to give students extra time in a center to work on their writing projects, but we do not recommend just assigning a personal narrative with little or no instruction. When students write within a genre, they should also read deeply within that genre to make the reading-writing connection even stronger. Students need time and instruction to develop as proficient writers and they need to understand their purposes for writing. This development requires the skillful support of a teacher.

We prefer the term *literacy options* for work that students complete independently. We use the term *option* rather than *station* or *center* to move away from the notion of rotation. Options don't have to be tied to a particular location, as students can bring their literacy option to a quiet location, eliminating the disruption of rotation. Students can choose from options on a chart (see list on following page) each day or week and create their own personal contract. For example, out of a list of five options, perhaps two must be completed and they can choose the third from among the other three. This way, they are empowered through having some personal choice, and you can make sure they complete important work. These literacy options should be presented to students with directions and expectations for engagement and completion. You and your students can amend the list of the following literacy options so it meets your class's particular interests and needs.

- Independent reading of core selection, choice selection; from themed library, leveled texts
- Paired reading
- Responding to literature selections in a reading journal
- Responding to reading through art or drama
- Listening center
- Reading to support writing project
- Poetry center (work with words and language of theme)
- Word study
- Fluency practice with leveled text
- Science or social studies connections

During small-group instruction, readers have a substantial amount of time where they are not working with the teacher directly. Be sure to make this time worthwhile for students and ask them to help create engaging literacy options. Independent work contracts are useful for classroom management and accountability. The contracts do not all need to be the same. Each child should personalize his or her contract and then review it with the teacher in a goal-setting meeting each week. For instance, students can list the options they will complete, along with a timeline for completion. In this manner, you still have control over the literacy options/centers, and your students learn about accountability, choices, and goal setting.

## Launching the Theme

### Concept Lesson—Challenges

For students to embrace the theme Challenges, they should have a rich understanding of what the concept means. We recommend conducting a concept lesson during which, as a class, you discover conceptions and misconceptions of the concept *challenges* (Obenchain & Morris, 2007). The word *challenges* means different things to different people in different contexts. The meaning changes with time and place, so to develop a deep understanding of the concept, students articulate as a whole class what it is and what it isn't. For example, one student may say, "It is getting my homework done," while another student who finds homework easy may disagree. This lesson serves as the foundation for the whole theme.

To begin the concept lesson, write the word *challenges* on the board or overhead. Have students brainstorm a list of words or phrases that describe the concept. They might come up with things like "homework," "science fair project," "getting along with my sister," "learning to do a lay-up," "running at soccer practice," "earning money," "having other nations get along," "making friends," "moving to another school," "being shy," "getting around if you are handicapped," "traveling to other countries," "learning something new," "getting all your work done," "helping out around the house," or "passing tests."

Then put students in groups of three and have them sort the list into categories. Provide an example or two from the list that your students create. Possible categories for this example list include:

- Attitudes
- Sports
- School
- Getting along
- Home
- Violence
- World challenges
- Contests

Following this process, provide students with excerpts from texts. From these examples, they can be guided to develop a list of the characteristics of challenges. For instance, they might decide that challenges can be frightening to an individual. Additionally, it is likely they will come to realize that there are similarities and differences in the way people think of the concept of *challenges*.

## Questioning vs. Discussion

Lastly, before extending the theme, we share some ideas on questioning versus discussion. In the core selection, *Miss Alaineus*, there are 27 questions that are recommended for teachers to ask while engaging with the reading—that's one to three questions per page. If teachers use all of these questions, then *they* are directing the flow of thinking. These questions are leading students to think in a particular way about the text. For example, one question asks, "What happens when Sage calls Starr to get the vocabulary words?" The answer requires only literal recall. The question is placed there as a comprehension *check* rather than a way to *develop* comprehension. Allow time for students to read and think about the story on their own first. The description of exemplary classrooms from the chapter's epigraph, "intellectual environments that produce not mere technical competence, but caring, secure, actively literate human beings," helps us remember that it is not just about skills, but about helping children become literate human beings. We should invite students into a discussion by asking them what they make of the story and what questions they have about it. Teach your students to ask these kinds of questions, ones that help them develop comprehension and understanding, rather than just replying to preconceived questions printed in a manual. Figure 3.1 provides a comparison of questioning and facilitating a discussion.

There are many ways to engage your students in discussion rather than have them play a guessing game in which they try to figure out the answer listed in the margin of the core program. Some of the questions can be very useful, but ask them after students have shared their interpretations and have made sense of the text themselves or with one another. It is far more powerful if we teach the *reader*, rather than just focusing on the reading selection.

### Figure 3.1: QUESTIONING vs. DISCUSSION

| Questioning | Discussion |
|---|---|
| Teacher asks questions with known answer. | Teacher facilitates by responding to questions posed by students. |
| Teacher controls who speaks. | Students ask questions of one another, building on one another's comments. |
| Teacher decides on the kinds of questions to ask. | Students share ideas and interpretations that make sense of the reading. |
| Teacher asks numerous questions to teach (test) comprehension. | Comprehension is monitored by students; they pose questions to make meaning. |
| Teacher decides what answers are acceptable. | Teachers and students ask questions they do not know the answers to and reflect on possible responses. |
| Teacher poses a question, one student responds, and another question is posed. | Teacher and students respond to one another in a conversational way, listening to one another. Frequently, the conversation does not include the teacher, but moves from student to student. |

# The Extended Literacy Curriculum

To extend the benchmark text, *Miss Alaineus*, we chose, first, to explore realistic fiction in which the main characters face a variety of challenges, and second, to conduct an investigation on story resolutions through text sets constructed from a variety of realistic fiction sub-themes. We selected these extensions because they highlight the main theme, and the genre of realistic fiction creates space for fifth graders to talk about real-world challenges and to analyze the resolutions presented by the authors of the various reading selections.

## Reading Connections

To begin, have the class consider the characteristics of realistic fiction and the criteria for choosing titles. Doing so helps young readers to think critically about the selections in a core reading program, as well as the selections they make throughout this theme and beyond. Anderson (2005, p. 204) presents the following characteristics and criteria for evaluating contemporary realistic fiction. We recommend thinking about them as you and your students select potential texts.

**Characteristics of contemporary realistic fiction:**
- Setting is in a modern time.
- Characters are realistic people.
- Often narrated in first person.
- Plot reflects real-life situations.
- Protagonist finds a way to cope with problems.
- Characters are the same age as their intended audience.

**Criteria for evaluating contemporary realistic fiction:**
- The topic is suitable for the age intended.
- The book tells a good story that children will enjoy.
- The plot is credible.
- The characters are convincing.
- The author avoids stereotyping.
- The theme emerges naturally from the story rather than being stated too obviously.
- The theme is worth imparting to children.
- The author avoids didacticism.

Even though we present these lists as finished products, it is more effective to construct a similar list with your students as you read a variety of titles and make note of what they have in common. As you and your students read *Miss Alaineus*, the benchmark text, attend to its essential characteristics. As you then read other titles, you can add to and revise the list together. There are many realistic fiction titles that focus on children who face a challenge they must overcome. You can make these titles available for independent reading, paired reading, or literature discussion groups (see Chapter 4 for more about these groups).

## Realistic Fiction Titles

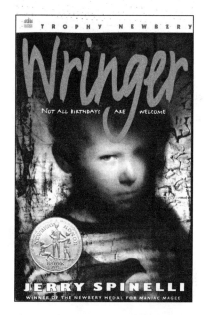

*Wringer* (Spinelli, 1997). This story is about a young boy named Palmer who lives in a town where they conduct an annual pigeon-shooting contest. When boys in this town turn 10, they are expected to become wringers—people who wring the necks of shot birds that haven't died. Palmer does not want to become a wringer, but is afraid of what others will say, especially the young boy gang into which he has been inducted. Palmer finds an unlikely pet pigeon, and an unlikely friend in the girl across the street named Dorothy. He must face the challenge of being who he wants to be, saving his pet pigeon, and maintaining his friendship with Dorothy. This is a great book for young readers as they contemplate the choices Palmer makes and compare them with their own lives.

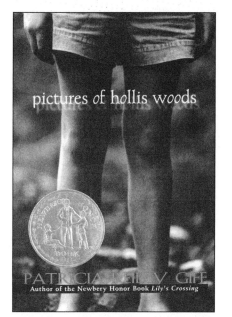

*Pictures of Hollis Woods* (Reilly-Giff, 2002). This is the story of a young girl named Hollis Woods who has been in and out of foster homes most of her young life. She finally finds a family, the Regans, who want her, yet she runs away from them, too. She ends up with an elderly woman, Josie, who takes her in but is beginning to lose her memory. Hollis works to keep this information from the social workers. All the while, she dreams of living again with the Regans. Josie must face the challenge of coming to terms with her past decisions and helping Josie to stay out of a nursing home. In the end she learns a lot about herself and those who love her.

*Olive's Ocean* (Henkes, 2003). This is another coming-of-age story about a young girl who must face her past actions and decisions. Martha, the main character, is visited by the mother of Olive, a little girl who just died. Olive's mother tells Martha of a journal entry Olive made before her fatal accident. In this entry Martha learns of Olive's wish to be friends with her and their common dream of becoming writers. As Olive becomes part of all that she thinks and does, Martha comes to terms with her own life on a family vacation as she faces the challenge of growing up and becoming who she wants to be.

*Frindle* (Clements, 2003). This is a fun story about a boy who takes on Mrs. Granger, his fifth-grade

English teacher. Nick Allen is famous for creating diversions at the end of each class to avoid having homework assigned. One day he tries it on Mrs. Granger, but it backfires, leading to an interesting vocabulary adventure. Nick takes on a challenge and invents the word *frindle* to replace the word *pen*. The new word becomes very popular, so popular that it receives national attention. All the while, Mrs. Granger and Nick battle each other for control. In the epilogue we learn that the word *frindle* made it into the dictionary and Mrs. Granger was always on Nick's side.

These titles are exceptional for literature study groups or for classroom read-alouds. The characters in these books all face real challenges and work through them in interesting ways.

The second extension is an investigation of story resolutions in children's literature and the media. We recommend putting students into small groups. Ask each group to either construct its own realistic-fiction text set or to choose a text set that has been put together by the teacher. Figure 3.2 lists examples of text sets that focus on families, literacy, diversity, school, and death and aging. Each text was chosen because the main characters face a challenge and the story comes to a unique resolution. The text sets are composed of three picture books and one chapter book. We also tried to vary the gender of the characters.

We highly recommend that you ask your students to help make the text sets with guidance from you. If students help to construct the sets, they become familiar with the genre and choose titles they are interested in reading. You can put suggested titles on the board for them to choose from, as well as provide them with lists of books and Web sites that recommend realistic fiction titles (nccde.org and www.librarybooklists.org provide lists organized by category).

### Figure 3.2: REALISTIC FICTION TEXT SETS

| Text Set 1<br><br>Families | Text Set 2<br><br>Literacy | Text Set 3<br><br>Diversity and Society | Text Set 4<br><br>School | Text Set 5<br><br>Death and Aging |
|---|---|---|---|---|
| *Piggybook* by Anthony Browne | *Read for Me, Mama* by Vashanti Rahaman | *Smoky Night* by Eve Bunting | *Crow Boy* by Taro Yashima | *The Tenth Good Thing About Barney* by Judith Viorst |
| *A Chair for My Mother* by Vera B. Williams | *The Wednesday Surprise* by Eve Bunting | *Voices in the Park* by Anthony Browne | *Yo! Yes?* by Chris Raschka | *Wilfrid Gordon McDonald Partridge* by Mem Fox |
| *When Sophie Gets Angry—Really, Really Angry* by Molly Bang | *More Than Anything Else* by Marie Bradby | *Allison* by Allen Say | *Love That Dog* by Sharon Creech | *Nana Upstairs & Nana Downstairs* by Tomie dePaola |
| *Walk Two Moons* by Sharon Creech | *Just Juice* by Karen Hesse | *Maniac McGee* by Jerry Spinelli | *Stargirl* by Jerry Spinelli | *Sun and Spoon* by Kevin Henkes |

Once the class has created its text sets, ask students to propose how they would like to go about reading the various selections, focusing on the literary element of resolution. For example, looking at the first text set in Figure 3.2, the mom in *Piggybook* leaves her family when they fail to help out around the house. Meanwhile, Sophie walks out of her house to cool down when she is really angry, and the mom in *Walk Two Moons* also walks out on her family when she feels she is not good enough for them. These three books have female characters who leave the family home to resolve their problems. These titles can be compared, in a comparison chart, with *A Chair for My Mother,* in which the mother works hard to purchase a chair for their home after they lose everything in a fire. Students can also focus on how those decisions influenced the rest of the family and other characters in the book. Each situation is unique, and students can look at the pros and cons of each character's decisions.

Students can then compare the resolutions they've charted to problems presented in the media. They can find news stories about people who were angry or sad in their situation and decided to resolve it by leaving. Teachers may want to organize students into small groups for these investigations. Once students have completed the tasks, teachers can combine groups for discussion centered on similarities and differences in outcomes. Students can compare these situations with their own lives. At right (Figure 3.3) is an example of a discussion guide for students to use. Again, we recommend involving students in the creation of these guide sheets.

## Figure 3.3: RESOLUTION GUIDE SHEET

### INVESTIGATION OF RESOLUTIONS

**Realistic Fiction Resolutions**

How do characters solve problems?

What do you think of the resolution?

Is it realistic to you?

Could you embrace it?

Do you see yourself or others doing the same?

**Media Resolutions**

How does the media portray resolutions?

What are the conflicts and resolutions presented?

Are they true or realistic?

Could you see yourself doing the same?

**Personal Resolutions**

How do you solve problems?

How does your family solve problems?

## Writing Connections

### Writing Extension 1: Poetry Anthology

To help children connect with the text sets that they've chosen or created, we recommend having them write and collect poetry on a realistic theme or topic of their choice. Focusing on poetry is a great way to engage students in reading and writing that is meaningful to them. If students are going to write poetry, they need to read it. You could create a poetry reading center as a literacy option during the reading block, as mentioned earlier in the chapter, or during writing workshop time. Either way, allow plenty of time for students to read and explore poetry selections. There are many great poetry anthologies written for children that focus on real-world topics.

Writing and collecting poetry can be a very engaging writing project for your students. First, have children read and explore poetry and make a hot topic list of possible themes for their anthology. Themes can be anything they like: friendship, love, pets, sports, death, family, colors, sibling rivalry, contests, news, and challenges. Once they have each chosen a theme, ask them to collect poetry on their theme to include in their anthologies. We recommend they each find five poems to include so that they have a variety. The

## SOME OF OUR FAVORITE POETRY ANTHOLOGIES

*All the Small Poems* by Valerie Worth

*The Butterfly Jar* by Jeff Moss

*A Family Book of Poetry* edited by Caroline Kennedy

*I Like You, If You Like Me: Poems About Friendship* edited by Myra Cohen Livingston

*If I Were in Charge of the World and Other Worries: Poems for Children and Their Parents* by Judith Viorst

*The New Kid on the Block* by Jack Prelutsky

*Night on Neighborhood Street* by Eloise Greenfield

*Poetry for Young People: American Poetry* edited by John Hollander

*Poetry for Young People: Maya Angelou* edited by Edwin Graves Wilson

*Poetry for Young People: Emily Dickinson* edited by Frances Schoonmaker

*Poetry for Young People: Robert Frost* edited by Gary Schmidt

*Poetry for Young People: Carl Sandburg* edited by Frances Schoonmaker

*Poetry for Young People: William Carlos Williams* edited by Christopher MacGowan & Robert Crockett

*Poetry Speaks to Children* edited by Elise Paschen

*The Random House Book of Poetry for Children* edited by Jack Prelutsky

*Sad Underwear and Other Complications: More Poems for Children and Their Parents* by Judith Viorst

*Sports Page* by Arnold Adoff

selections must be purposeful to the students and reflect their interpretation of their themes. Require students to write poems (two to five) that reflect their theme as well. Last, we recommend having students write an about-the-author page and a page that offers an explanation of why each poem has been included. As they write about themselves and their selections, they make connections to the core theme and the reading they have been doing, and think critically about why they chose and wrote their selections of poetry. These anthologies are powerful and allow children to showcase their own poetry next to poetry they admire. Have a poetry celebration with snacks and invited guests and ask students to recite their published poems.

## Writing Extension 2: Responding to Realistic Fiction

Throughout this unit, students are reading a wide variety of genres connected to the core theme, Challenges. Certainly, the core program provides a large selection of work sheets for students to respond to. However, we suggest students use reader response journals instead. They allow students to respond to literature in a much more open-ended and engaging way. We recommend using spiral-bound notebooks or even having students make special Challenges response journals reinforced with plastic combs. The idea is for students to write and collect their reflections. When they respond on worksheets that are graded and returned, there is a lack of connection between the assignments. Children lose them and rarely return to them to reflect on the progress of their responses. In a spiral-bound notebook, responses are in order, kept safely (for the most part), and belong to the students. Teachers are free to have students look back at an earlier response, and it's easier for students to make connections between books.

Students can record their ideas in a variety of ways in their journals (described below). Teachers respond to the students in writing rather than with a grade. Too often, students spend a considerable amount of time on a worksheet only to get it back with red marks and a grade, neither of which enhances their comprehension. Not everything children do needs to be graded! We cannot emphasize that enough. When young readers are thinking about what they read and formulating ideas, they need to feel free to experiment with ideas and to interpret the literature in new ways. If their work is always graded for correct responses, they stop taking chances and only read for that correct answer, rather than critically. With that said, we provide descriptions of some responses students could explore in their journals after reading any of the core reading selections or extended literacy selections. We use the benchmark text, *Miss Alaineus*, as an example in each one.

**Multigenre Writing.** Students could think carefully about one of the characters and imagine what kind of writing would be important to him or her, or imagine some kind of writing that another character might write about him or her. *Example:* Sage could write a journal entry describing her feelings after being humiliated in class. Or Sage might create an entry in the school program describing her vocabulary word and costume.

**Dialogue Journal.** There are many options for a dialogue journal. A student could write about the story to another student, the teacher, or a parent, and have that person respond. A variation would be for a student to have two characters in the story write back and forth about their feelings about a specific event in the story. Or students could dialogue after the story ended, providing a kind of epilogue. *Example:* A student writes a conversation between Sage and Starr.

**Music or Art With Written Explanation.** Students could find or create a piece of music that resembles the flow or meaning of the story. This would really connect with the poetry anthology; students could include a song in their collection along with poems. Students could sing or play the piece of music or include the words in their response log. After they choose a piece of music, students could respond in writing about what the song represents and how it helps them to interpret the reading at a deeper level. Similarly, students could create or find artwork that enhances their interpretation of the text or expresses how they feel about the story or topic. They could include a written explanation of how and why these pieces connect and express their interpretation. *Example:* Students find music that accompanies Sage on stage when she presents her Miss Alaineus robe. Then students explain how the music goes with the character and her actions.

**Impressions, Connections, and Wonderings.** In their journals, students could share impressions and ideas they have about the book, what they notice about events and important details, and how these impact their overall understanding (Serafini & Serafini-Youngs, 2006). Then they make literary and/or personal connections to the text and explain how these help them understand the book at a deeper level. Lastly, students share wonderings or questions they have about the text and/or the worldly connections they might be making. *Example:* Students share personal connections about being humiliated in front of their friends, express their impressions of how Sage solved her problems, and share questions they have of how that solution would work in their own classroom with their peers.

**Review.** Students write a book review and then submit it to Amazon.com or other places that accept children's reviews of books. Students need to read some reviews, understand the format, and then write up their own opinion of the book.

**Questions and Quiz.** Students answer some of the questions that are provided in the core text or on some of the work sheets. You could type the questions up or put them on the board and students could choose which two or three questions to answer after reading the selection. You might even ask them to create their own core program questions. Show students the list of questions the program recommends asking and have them create their own questions and then explain why they are good questions for that story or text selection. *Example:* Compare Sage to another character or person you have read about recently. How has Sage changed in the story?

These are only a few examples of what children could write about in a reader response journal. The key word is *response*, meaning response by the child and response by the teacher. The most important aspect of these journals is for students to respond to their reading in an open-ended way so they may explore their own interpretations and then for the teacher to respond to—rather than grade—their ideas. When the teacher responds in the journal, she is able to push the student further in her thinking, sharing insights about the reading process as she is teaching to the student's needs. When notebooks are graded and corrected, learning stops because students are no longer reflecting on how to expand their ideas. We recommend dividing the class into five groups and collecting from each group once a week so you can read a collection of their responses and help them expand their ideas on a regular basis. Or students may mark one response that they want you to respond to, limiting the number of entries you need to respond to; the drawback with this option is that you won't see how their thinking develops. These are a few ways to manage the response notebook so you are not overwhelmed and can enjoy the comments your students provide.

## Author or Illustrator Study

Eve Bunting makes a wonderful author to study. She has written more than 200 books for young readers over the last 30 years, extensively within the contemporary realistic fiction genre. Because she has written about contemporary topics over time, it would be interesting to compare some of her earlier works, like *One More Flight*, published in 1976, about a boy who runs away from a foster home and befriends a man who cares for birds, to later ones, like *My Red Balloon*, published in 2006, about a boy who waits for his father to return after being at sea for many months. Through this comparison, students could attend to the challenges children faced in the 1970s and how they might be different from and similar to those they face today.

She also makes a great author to study because she has written chapter books and picture books with a wide variety of illustrators. You can look at how the different styles of illustrations enhance the stories she tells. Bunting writes from the perspective of an Irish immigrant and empathizes with those who have faced the same challenges. She shares her never-ending quest to tell the stories of children from around the world who have faced challenges. At right is a selected list of her books for study.

## Vocabulary Extensions

To begin this themed investigation, we focus on two key words: *challenge* and *resolution*. Each of these words has been used as a foundation for many of the reading activities thus far. In this exploration, we focus on the meaning of the words that subsequent curricular activities build upon.

## Word Exploration

Write the two targeted words, *challenge* and *resolution*, on index cards and place them on the wall so you can make a visual web. Invite teams of students to find various definitions for the words and write sentences that help others understand the words. Students use in-class and online dictionaries, such as the one mentioned in Chapter 2 (www.ldoceonline.com). Students work on the guide sheet (see Figure 3.4, next page) independently and then collaborate in small groups to share their answers. The groups put various definitions, examples, sentences, and illustrations up on the word wall for the rest of the class to learn from. Each group takes its turn to present its information to the class, so everyone can record new information on their own sheets.

## EVE BUNTING BOOKS

### Picture Books

*A Day's Work*

*The Butterfly House*

*December*

*Fly Away Home*

*Going Home*

*Market Day*

*The Memory String*

*My Red Balloon*

*One Green Apple*

*A Picnic in October*

*Rudi's Pond*

*Smoky Night*

*Some Frog!*

*The Wall*

*The Wednesday Surprise*

### Chapter Books

*Is Anybody There?*

*One More Flight*

*Nasty Stinky Sneakers*

*Our Sixth Grade Sugar Babies*

*Our Sixth Grade Sleepover*

*The Summer of Riley*

**Figure 3.4: VOCABULARY GUIDE SHEET**

Word Work

Challenge/Resolution

Definitions:

Synonyms:

Sentences:

Where would you use the word?

Examples from the text:

Illustrations:

## Personal Journal

We also recommend that students use a journal to keep track of interesting words they come across in their reading. During a literature study group, one of the first items of business is to go over new and interesting words and confusing ones. Students can keep track of these words easily in their reader response journals by dedicating some pages at the end for a vocabulary focus and for new words they would like to add to the whole-class word wall.

## Vocabulary Parade

In the spirit of *Miss Alaineus*, you could have a vocabulary parade. Students work with various definitions of *challenge* and *resolution*, and perhaps other key words from the theme. Then they illustrate or dress up like their vocabulary word and parade in their own class or in others. It's a great activity to share with reading buddies or at a parent night.

## Ties to Content Areas Such as Social Studies and Science

Ties between the theme of Challenges and science and social studies are wide and varied. There are connections that can be made to the natural world and to your own community. In this section, we describe ways your students can take an active stance toward the words *challenge* and *resolution*.

### Science/Health/Math

A great opportunity for you to promote good eating habits and physical fitness is to create a physical fitness challenge using the Presidential Physical Fitness Challenge, which can be found online at www.presidentschallenge.org. This Web site walks you through setting up, managing, and maintaining a physical fitness challenge. It also offers online activity logs for students to track their progress; you sign your class up as a group, and then enter each student's information so they can track their progress and make connections to their home activities as well. At a time when physical education classes are being cut, this core theme extension provides a great opportunity for real-world reading, math activities, use of technology, and, the best benefit of all, learning how to work toward a healthy lifestyle.

Each student completes the first round of physical fitness activities and records his or her efforts as a baseline. Then they can track changes in their endurance and activity levels over time. As a class you could read about the importance of being physically active and eating a balanced diet (see related Web sites on next page). Students record what they eat for a week and how much time they spend watching TV, playing video games, and working on the computer and compare that to the amount of time they spend being active. Then, they challenge one another to eat healthier and move more as they complete the physical fitness activities and chart their progress each week. This could be a whole-class science experiment!

Students record their progress on charts, which makes for a great math connection. They determine the scale they need for their charts and learn about line graphs to show progress over time. Students also learn how to put the information into an Excel spreadsheet to create computer-generated graphs for an authentic technology connection. On the next page you will find some related Web sites that provide information on nutrition, physical fitness, and other healthy challenges for kids.

## HEALTHY KIDS WEB SITES

| | |
|---|---|
| www.healthiergeneration.org | The Alliance for a Healthier Generation, in conjunction with Rachel Ray and Bill Clinton, asks children to take the Go Healthy Challenge. The site includes information on healthy eating habits and how to get physically active every day. There are quizzes for students to take and suggestions for beginning the initiative not just in your own classroom but also within your school. There are forms for your students to use to communicate with the school's food-services provider and the physical education teacher (if you have one) on how to rally the school behind a school-wide Go Healthy Challenge. |
| www.education-world.com | This Web site provides numerous suggestions and a physical fitness plan for students to follow, as well as descriptions of exercises for you and your students. |
| www.keepkidshealthy.com | This Web site is filled with information on how to establish healthy eating habits as well as a physical fitness routine. It describes a variety of exercises, from warm-ups to strength training, to help children create a routine that works for them. It includes a quiz for students to take to compare the amount of time they watch TV or play on the computer with the amount of time they exercise each day. |
| www.americanheart.org | The American Heart Association has wonderful links to material that promotes children's health and fitness. There are numerous articles and links for teachers and parents to use as a guide for a healthier lifestyle. The site has exercise ideas and healthy eating ideas, too. |

## Social Studies

A natural connection to the theme is to continue investigation of the word *resolution*. Rather than reading about resolutions in books, students connect making a resolution to the Go Healthy Challenge.

Students take the challenge school-wide by creating a campaign for a healthier lifestyle. First, the class has a meeting to brainstorm possible obstacles to instituting this challenge school-wide. They may decide to pilot-test such a campaign within their own classroom to find out the real obstacles, rather than just developing a campaign from their predictions.

Students might return to their essential/nonessential list and example/non-example chart and identify ideas that are specific to this healthy challenge and their school community. Using these ideas as a base, help students identify the top three challenges to instituting such a campaign. Next, students create a survey to ask other classes what they think about a school-wide physical fitness challenge campaign, and for ideas on how to implement it. Clearly, an interview with the principal would be necessary, and if you have a P. E. teacher, ask her for suggestions and find ways to get her involved.

To begin the campaign, students act as teachers, going into other classrooms to promote the Go Healthy Challenge. They demonstrate the program and the procedures. The Web sites we list on page 68 provide guidance for one class to make changes within their whole school. This would be a great social studies extension, as students focus on social activism and making a difference in their own local community.

## Visual Literacy Extensions and Technology Connections

### Media Analysis

In this activity, students research various media (broadcast media, print media, and the Internet) to see how each treats the same topic or issue. They then engage in critical discussions on what each media mode can and cannot do. As a final presentation, students create a "talk radio show" to discuss their different perspectives on the topic.

In order for students to *truly* understand the elements of design and the characteristics and constraints of any mode of media, they should work within that mode. So, we recommend taking the project one step further by having a team of students design advertisements or information for the Go Healthy Challenge campaign. They need to experiment with print, art, Web design, broadcast radio and television, photography, magazine articles, and newsletters. The challenge is to launch a campaign that uses a variety of modes to truly explore how these modes share meaning differently.

Students could experiment with video, editing, and the characteristics of the broadcast mode to create a commercial they could play for other classes. They could design a morning announcement or radio commercial for the school to play over the loudspeaker. By analyzing the media mode they're working with, they determine what elements (verbal, visual, etc.) they need to communicate their message effectively. A number of art extensions will emerge from this work, as students create posters using elements of design (described in Chapter 4). A whole-class comparison chart of the various modes serves as a great instructional/learning tool. These connections are a win-win situation—students learn about media, and empower themselves by participating in something great for themselves and for their school community.

# Connections to Fifth-Grade Literacy Standards

In Chapter 1, we shared the national standards presented by the International Reading Association and the National Council of Teachers of English. For this theme of study, the following national standards have been addressed: standards 1, 3, 4, 5, 6, 7, 8, 11, and 12.

For this theme we chose to look at the Minnesota State Department of Education language arts standards, which can be found at http://education.state.mn.us.

These standards are broken down into the following categories: reading and literature; writing; and speaking, listening, and viewing. We list the standards that are met or exceeded in the Challenges unit.

## Reading and Literature

### Word Recognition, Analysis, and Fluency
- The student will decode unfamiliar words using phonetic and structural analysis and will read with fluency and expression.

### Vocabulary Expansion
- The student will use a variety of strategies to expand reading, listening, and speaking vocabularies; acquire, understand, and use new vocabulary through explicit instruction as well as independent reading.

### Comprehension
- The student will understand the meaning of texts using a variety of strategies and will demonstrate literal, interpretive, inferential, and evaluative comprehension.

### Literature
- The student will actively engage in the reading process and read, understand, respond to, analyze, interpret, evaluate, and appreciate a wide variety of fiction, poetic, and nonfiction texts.

## Writing

### Types of Writing

- The student will compose various pieces of writing.

### Elements of Composition

- The student will engage in a writing process, with attention to organization, focus, quality of ideas, audience, and a purpose.

### Spelling, Grammar, and Usage

- The student will apply standard English conventions when writing.

## Speaking, Listening, and Viewing

- The student will demonstrate understanding and communicate effectively through listening and speaking.

### Media Literacy

- The student will critically analyze information found in electronic and print media, and will use a variety of these sources to learn about a topic and represent ideas, as well as identify distinctions in how information is presented in print and non-print materials (Minnesota Academic Standards Committee, 2003).

It is only through the blending of both core program and literature-based curricula that you can cover all these standards; neither one would do it alone. Moreover, by using both, you have facilitated students to enjoy and more deeply understand their reading and writing experiences.

## CHAPTER 4

# $S$ixth-Grade Possibilities

*$T$he power of genre instruction and multi-genre writing opens avenues that help teach-ers create rich lessons and learning events that are embedded in authentic learning.*

—Suzette Youngs and Diane Barone (2007)

The epigraph quoted above leads to one of the extensions we share in this chapter—one that pro-vides opportunities for teachers and students to explore genre in multiple ways, including a multi-genre writing experience. To explore sixth-grade possibilities, we chose the Houghton Mifflin core reading program (2005) and selected Theme 5, Doers and Dreamers. With its genre focus on speeches, the theme lends itself to many enriching opportunities for expansion and deep explo-ration. We offer many possibilities for teachers as there are too many choices for a teacher to use with one class. We believe it is important for you to critically analyze each learning activity as you match learners with activities. The activities should be personally meaningful to the students and should build a deeper understanding of the core theme.

## The Core Reading Program

Doers and Dreamers focuses on autobiographies and biographies to explore the lives of five people who have served as inspirational models for many others. The texts include *A Kind of Grace* by Jackie Joyner-Kersee; *Under the Royal Palms* by Alma Flora Ada; *Chuck Close Up Close* by Jan Greenberg; *Yolanda's Genius* by Carol Fenner; and *No Ordinary Baby: Wolfgang Amadeus Mozart* by Kathleen Krull. The text selections also highlight the genre of speech through the following: Abraham Lincoln's Gettysburg Address; *A Story of Courage, Bravery, Strength, and Heroism* by Shao Lee; Jerry Spinelli's Newbery acceptance speech; a commencement speech by Katherine Ortega; and an excerpt from Martin Luther King Jr.'s "I Have a Dream" speech. The selections were chosen to inspire children to dream and to provide models for them so they can accomplish their own goals.

We chose *A Kind of Grace* by Jackie Joyner-Kersee as the benchmark text for this theme. This autobiography of an American female athlete is a great example of the genre. Joyner-Kersee tells the story of how she became a heptathlon gold medalist in the 1992 Summer Olympics. She shares the obstacles she had to overcome as a little girl, during a time when organized sports for girls were nonexistent. Her coach had faith in her and helped her develop her talents and live her dreams. This autobiography follows a typical narrative structure, with the subject overcoming adversity to go on and achieve her goals. The book includes captioned photos of Jackie Joyner-Kersee that span from her childhood to the present.

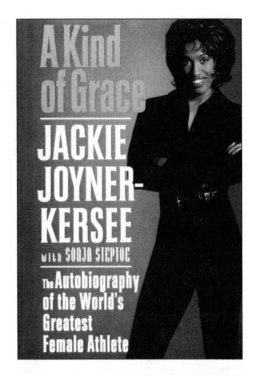

The goal is not just for students to learn about Jackie Joyner-Kersee but for them to become critical readers of autobiographies and biographies. Assigning biographies or autobiographies can disengage students if the expectation is simply to memorize a list of dates and important events in the subject's life. However, if students understand that reading an autobiography closely helps them understand the importance of people considered to be doers and dreamers, they develop a more complex way to view individuals. This understanding leads them to make personal connections through reading about and reflecting on these individuals. For example, reading about Jackie Joyner-Kersee's losses might help a student better understand the anger she feels when she loses a race—and how best to deal with it. Therefore, the focus of this chapter is more on the genre than on the benchmark text itself.

*A Kind of Grace* is the first reading selection in this theme and sets the tone for thinking about Doers and Dreamers. The core reading program addresses many specific skills and strategies with this single text and its corresponding leveled texts. The list that follows describes what is expected of students as they read this text.

## Comprehension

- Students create a KWL chart before, during, and after reading.
- They focus on summarizing various parts of her story.
- They set a purpose for reading.

- They are introduced to the idea of propaganda.
- They use compare and contrast to analyze events in her life.
- They use a questioning strategy to think about important events in her life.
- They sequence events to order and discuss the plotline of her story.
- They apply cause and effect reasoning to think critically about how Jackie succeeded.
- They make judgments about Jackie's actions throughout her life.

## Word Knowledge

### Phonics/Decoding

- Students focus on compound words like *counterclockwise*. They are reminded to look for the parts of words they recognize, sound them out, then look the word up in the dictionary.

### Vocabulary

- Students use their knowledge of the roots *ven* and *graph* to learn new words such as *geography*, *avenue*, and *autograph*.
- They focus on the endings and become familiar with words such as *conditioning*, *consoling*, *discouraged*, *endurance*, *sessions*, *sprints*, *squad*, and *unconventional*.
- They attend to antonyms to sharpen their writing. Students work with antonym pairs such as *slow* and *swift*, *thin* and *thick*.
- They explore words with multiple meanings and compare two different definitions with words such as *exercise*, *positive*, and *fantastic*.

### Spelling

- Students focus on final sounds (advert*ise*, organi*ze*, act*ive*, trag*ic* and signat*ure*).
- They read and spell the following words: *advertise*, *serious*, *tragic*, *positive*, *fantastic*, *active*, and *exercise*.

## Fluency

- Students focus on fluency as they reread selected parts of the text, either alone or with a partner.

## Writing

- Students complete four writing projects: a clarification composition, a how-to paragraph, a summary, and a speech.
- They participate in a writer's workshop to create a personal essay through six phases of the writing process: prewriting, drafting, revising, editing, proofreading, and publishing.

- They focus their efforts on voice and sentence fluency in their work with the 6 Traits. As students revise their story, they are asked to practice being precise and working with pronouns.
- They are given multiple graphic organizers to help them think about and organize their writing.

Clearly, that's a lot of learning expectations and instructional strategies for just one text. As stated in previous chapters, it is important to understand that the publishers of this core program did not intend for teachers to use every suggested activity. To do so would overwhelm you and your students. There just isn't enough time. We recommend that you review the suggestions, the work sheets, and the questions offered in the teacher's guide and analyze their usefulness and appropriateness for your students. Often, you can reduce the number of questions and limit the use of worksheets to only those that are most essential. Consider the following suggestions (Serafini & Giorgis, 2003) about questions to ask while you're reading and sharing a book with students:

- How often do students ask questions?
- What is the ratio between the amount of time the teacher talks and the amount of time students talk?
- Analyze questions and limit questions to those that lead to inquiry and important conversation about text.
- Allow children to read first and formulate their own questions and ideas, then come back for whole-group discussion.
- Turn some questions into statements.
- Don't ask questions to which you already know the answers.

These suggestions provide ways of thinking about the questions provided in a core program or those you develop yourself. It's important to remember that these questions are just a means to developing rich discussion and furthering student comprehension.

## Launching the Theme

To launch this unit, we recommend taking a few days to explore the theme, Doers and Dreamers, before engaging with the core text.

Because each suggestion we provide for launching the theme is grounded in literature discussion groups, we take a brief detour focused on establishing and supporting literature discussion groups before sharing them. If literature discussion groups are new to you, we encourage you to do some professional reading in this area with teachers in your grade level or from other grade levels, and to collaboratively implement literature discussion groups so that you can support one another. We also highly recommend audio- or videotaping your first literature discussions to analyze the process and your involvement with each group. These tapes can be shared with colleagues or, better yet, with students, to reflect on content and procedure. To help you get started, we have found some titles that match the theme and support literature discussion groups (see box below).

## BOOKS THAT PROMOTE DISCUSSION

### Picture books

*Amelia and Eleanor Go for a Ride* by Pam Muñoz-Ryan

*Baseball Saved Us* by Ken Mochizuki

*Duke Ellington: The Piano Prince and His Orchestra* by Andrea Davis Pinkney

*The Dream Keeper and Other Poems* by Langston Hughes

*Gleam and Glow* by Eve Bunting

*Horace and Morris but Mostly Dolores* by Eve Bunting

*Miss Rumphius* by Eve Bunting

*A Picture Book of Amelia Earhart* by David Adler

*One Candle* by Eve Bunting

*Owl Moon* by Jane Yolen

*Read for Me, Mama* by Vashanti Rahaman

*Rose Blanche* by Roberto Innocenti

*Smoky Night* by Eve Bunting

*Something Permanent* by Cynthia Rylant

*Starry Messenger* by Peter Sis

*The Story of Ferdinand* by Munro Leaf

*The Straight Line Wonder* by Eve Bunting

*Sylvester and the Magic Pebble* by William Steig

*Tea with Milk* by Alan Say

*The Wednesday Surprise* by Eve Bunting

### Chapter Books

*Becoming Naomi* by Pam Muñoz-Ryan

*Catherine Called Birdy* by Karen Cushman

*Dominic* by William Steig

*Esperanza Rising* by Pam Muñoz-Ryan

*Flipped* by Wendy Van Draanen

*Flying Solo* by Ralph Fletcher

*Frindle* by Andrew Clements

*The Giver* by Lois Lowry

*Just Juice* by Karen Hesse

*Love That Dog* by Sharon Creech

*Parallel Journeys* by Eleanor Ayer

*Seedfolks* by Paul Fleischman

*Stargirl* by Jerry Spinelli

*Tale of Despereaux* by Kate DiCamillo

*The Wanderer* by Sharon Creech

A great place to incorporate these literature discussion groups would be during a second literacy block. Choose four or five book selections, perhaps from those listed previously, or have students choose them and then place them on the chalkboard ledge. You might give a brief talk on each book to create motivation for student selection and reading. Then allow students a few days to peruse the books. Following this, place a sticky note on the cover of each book. Students can then sign up by writing their name on the sticky note of the book they prefer to read. After students have signed up for a literature study group, make plans to meet with each group, introduce the group's chosen book, and set an agenda that includes a timeline for reading and any other expectations. Meet two to three times per week with each group, depending on the group's needs. Your role is to read along with them, meet with them, and facilitate conversations as a member (not the leader) of the group. Read, meet, and discuss until the book is completed and then meet afterward to discuss themes and interesting aspects of the text. Now, we know some of you are thinking that to read four or five books is too much with your current teaching load. So, here are some options:

- Read and meet with only two groups
- Allow the other groups to read without you, but meet with them to facilitate their meeting
- Allow groups to read and meet without you, but have them respond in their reader response journals so you may respond to them
- Read and meet with all groups on a flexible schedule

There are numerous ways to engage readers with independent reading and discussion. The important aspect to remember is that most of the reading required by the core program is on-demand reading; in other words, it's done on the spot. Students do not take home the anthology, read the passage, take notes, mull it over, and then come back the next day to share their interpretation. That makes independent reading crucial for students to truly develop as critical readers. Most teachers require students to read independently at home and record the minutes read in their reading journals. What we suggest, however, is to connect the two. In this manner, as they read at home, students make connections to the theme and reading strategies they've learned during the day.

Establishing literature discussion groups before, or as part of, launching the theme gives students a few weeks to read and discuss the various books, which should be plenty of time to read, explore, and investigate the various selections. Students naturally begin to make connections, as both literacy blocks and at-home reading are focusing on the same theme and strategies.

Now we return to suggestions for a theme launch. A great way to introduce the theme is to have students read and discuss poetry (Serafini & Serafini-Youngs, 2006), as poems are short and provide students with the opportunity to practice sharing ideas. A wonderful poet to begin with is Langston Hughes, in particular his poetry book for children, *The Dream Keeper* (1996). This book is filled with thought-provoking poems about how children, especially children of color, hold tight to their dreams. We recommend choosing one poem and making copies for the entire class. You might begin with "The Dream Keeper," which is closely tied to our theme.

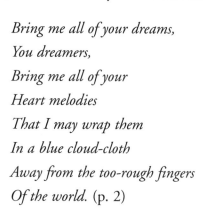

> *Bring me all of your dreams,*
> *You dreamers,*
> *Bring me all of your*
> *Heart melodies*
> *That I may wrap them*
> *In a blue cloud-cloth*
> *Away from the too-rough fingers*
> *Of the world.* (p. 2)

Then, in small, heterogeneous groups, have students discuss the poem and write—right on their copies—their thoughts, questions, and ideas about the poem. Give them a few moments to take in the poem before recording any ideas. When they're done, ask them to discuss their ideas in small groups. You might have the groups record their ideas on chart paper so they may share and compare with other groups. As students are discussing, you can move around the room and eavesdrop on their conversations. You might record some interesting insights as well as confusions to share with them later. Also, take notes on the process of the discussions and always be on the lookout for "helpers and blockers," those students who support and extend dialogue or those who stop or disrupt it (Serafini & Serafini-Youngs, 2006, p. 8). Share your observations and interpretations with students as a member of the group. Your comments should not dominate the conversations, but rather nudge them further than they would have gone on their own. Peterson and Eeds (2007) refer to this as "shooting literary arrows" (p. 10).

Then, bring students back to a whole-group discussion, where each group can discuss its interpretations and you as the teacher can also contribute. The important aspect of this structure is that students have had a chance to consider the piece before you or the program dictate the direction they are expected to take. You can now teach reading strategies specific to poetry that you noticed students need, and build on the foundation of understanding they have just constructed.

A second way to launch the theme involves creating a Doers and Dreamers class chart. Ask students to think about "The Dream Keeper" and how it might reveal aspects of dreamers. Students might consider: What does Langston Hughes want us to think about dreamers? The next day, you might choose different poems from Langston Hughes, or you might invite students to find poetry that they feel relates to the theme. Their responses can be added to the chart and considered and reflected upon as they move through this theme.

To stimulate conversation, you might try a goldfish bowl strategy (Raphael, Pardo, & Highfield, 2002). Choose three or four students who exhibit excellent literature discussion group strategies, sit with them in the middle of the room, and have a conversation about a particular poem while the rest of the class sits on the outside of the circle. The students on the outside act as researchers—analyzing the conversation and behaviors of those on the inside and discussing what they've heard and how it was talked about. Then have the whole group discuss what happened and unpack what makes a good literature discussion. The list in Figure 4.1 suggests some details of what an expert literature discussion group might look and sound like. Please note that the list pertains to all text genres, not only to poetry.

A third way to launch the theme is to create a classroom graffiti wall. Students can write quotes on it, place covers of books that enhance the theme, write down their own dreams, record things they do for the community, put up famous paintings and photos of dreamers and doers, and hang their own artwork that embodies the essence of the theme. The wall acts as a central focus for the theme that can be added to on a daily basis.

**Figure 4.1: ELEMENTS OF A LITERATURE DISCUSSION**

## Preparation

Read the text and prepare to discuss the following:

- Bring text to group
- Use sticky notes to mark important passages
- Prepare written response
- Share discussion ideas

## Process of Discussion

- Share opinions of the book
- Share personal experiences/connections
- Talk about what you did not understand
- Make sure everyone participates
- Ask questions
- Take notes
- Stay on task and topic
- Take turns with speaking
- Create some responses with group members in mind
- Introduce new ideas

## Analysis

- Share what you loved and hated
- Share things that puzzle you
- Consider diverse viewpoints
- Form questions about the text for you and your group to discuss
- Think about either a profound question or observation about the text and/or the illustrations
- Share how the book relates to each person in the group
- Critique positive and negative aspects
- Use literary elements and understanding of text structure to analyze text
- Find worldly connections
- Respond personally
- Defend ideas with examples
- Extend ideas rather than just notice elements

# The Extended Literacy Curriculum

To extend this benchmark text, we have chosen to look at biographical picture books of men and women who have made a difference in American history. We chose this extension because it highlights the genre of biographies through books that tell stories in both pictures and words.

## Reading Connections

### Informational Text (Biographies and Autobiographies)

There are many beautiful picture book biographies of inspirational figures from our nation's history. In this chapter we provide brief summaries of a few that might help you get started with your investigation of the theme, Doers and Dreamers. We also emphasize historical fiction and fictionalized biographies. These books are based on real events and people, but various aspects have been fictionalized to tell a complete story that goes beyond the limitations of the historical record. We recommend reading some of these aloud to your whole class and making the other titles available for students to read independently or in pairs. As students read these selections, they can share and extend the core theme with their classmates.

*Martin's Big Words* (Rappaport, 2001). This is an amazing picture book about the words of Martin Luther King Jr. Bryan Collier uses a multitude of collage and painting techniques to illustrate the book. He varies the perspective and colors to visually represent powerful and moving events in King's life. The author's and illustrator's notes are exquisite and explain the process, purpose, and meaning of many illustrations and words in the text.

*The Librarian of Basra* (Winter, 2005). Alia Muhammad Baker was a librarian in Basra, Iraq. For many years, her library was an important place to meet and housed a collection of 30,000 books. During the Iraq war, the bombing threatened her library, so she began to empty the library of all its books, storing them in unique hiding places away from the eyes of the public and soldiers. The story is about how a community worked together to help Alia preserve the collection and also sheds light on a unique perspective of the Iraq war.

*When Marian Sang* (Ryan, 2002). Brian Selznick creates a beautiful celebration of the color brown in this emotional picture book about Marian Anderson, the first African American to

sing at the Metropolitan Opera House. The images and text capture her struggle, and the story flows as beautifully as the music. The story begins with her childhood and ends with her historic performances at the Lincoln Memorial and with the Metropolitan Opera.

*Snowflake Bentley* (Briggs Martin, 1998). *Snowflake Bentley*, a picture book illustrated in woodcuts and hand-tinted with watercolors, tells the story of a scientist, Willie Bentley, who photographed snowflakes to study their unique formations and to show that no two are alike.

*Amelia and Eleanor Go for a Ride* (Ryan, 1999). This story is about the friendship between two of the most influential woman in American history—Amelia Earhart and

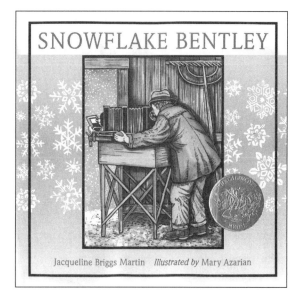

Eleanor Roosevelt—and the time they spent together. Eleanor invites Amelia to the White House for dinner, and when a reporter mentions to Amelia that Eleanor has just received her student pilot license, Amelia offers to teach her how to fly. In fact, they take off on a historic night flight to Baltimore and back. When they return, Eleanor gives Amelia a ride in her new sports car. Illustrator Brian Selznick used colored pencil and crayon to create dazzling illustrations that illuminate the story.

A few more we like:

David Adler's *A Picture Book of Lewis and Clark*
David Adler's *Joe Louis: America's Fighter*
Diane Stanley's *Michelangelo*
Diane Stanley's *Joan of Arc*

An important element of the picture-book biography genre is how text and illustrations work together to tell a person's story. The story could not exist without the illustrations and vice versa. Text is treated as an important graphic element and careful attention is paid to its placement. These books not only extend the core theme of Doers and Dreamers, but also provide an avenue for teachers and students to explore visual literacy.

These books span various genres, but they are connected by the theme, Doers and Dreamers. As in the benchmark text, *A Kind of Grace*, these texts focus on people or characters that actively follow their dreams. They find a way to live their dreams as they overcome many challenges along the way. As a

## OTHER BOOKS FOR EXPLORATION

### Historical Fiction or Fictionalized Biographies

*More Than Anything Else* by Marie Bradby

*Thank You Sarah: The Woman Who Saved Thanksgiving* by Laurie Halse Anderson

*Sister Anne's Hands* by Marybeth Loribecki

*The Bracelet* by Yoshiko Uchida

*Pish, Posh, Said Hieronymus Bosch* by Nancy Willard

*Show Way* by Jacqueline Woodson

### Fantasy

*Jungle Drums* by Graeme Base

*Koala Lou* by Mem Fox

*Tuesday* by David Weisner

*Seven Blind Mice* by Ed Young

class, you could create a comparison chart to look at how each character met his or her goals and what actions they took to reach them. You could also look at themes, both explicit and implicit, that pair with the Doers and Dreamers theme. Certainly the core text selections, as well as *Under the Royal Palm, Chuck Close Up Close,* and *No Ordinary Baby: Wolfgang Amadeus Mozart,* could all be analyzed closely and compared with many of the classroom titles. The core program offers a comparison chart, but it needs to be expanded to incorporate more critical questions as well as to make room for characteristics students want to compare across titles and genres. Figure 4.2 shares a chart that could be used to evaluate biographies.

### Figure 4.2: GENRE COMPARISON CHART

| | Autobiography | Biography | Historical Fiction/ Fictionalized Biography | Fantasy |
|---|---|---|---|---|
| How do characters meet their goals? | | | | |
| Why is their story important to tell? | | | | |
| Is the story believable? | | | | |
| Does the story cover positive and negative attributes? | | | | |
| Can you identify with him or her? | | | | |
| Is the story accurate? | | | | |
| What are the character's limitations? | | | | |

The chart serves merely as an avenue to meaning and discussion, not as an end in itself. You might want to consider such charts as a checkpoint for understanding rather than as a way to generate grades. What do the students understand? What are they confusing? These charts create a space for students to discuss the value, validity, and usefulness of these genres in their lives.

## Kinds of biographies

There are four divisions that we use to categorize biographies.

**Complete biographies** cover the entire life of the person. They tend to be much longer than the other types. These books are typically at a higher reading level. Russell Freedman's are particularly good:

> *Lincoln: A Photobiography*
> *Eleanor Roosevelt: A Life of Discovery*
> *The Voice That Challenged the Nation: Marian Anderson and the Struggle for Equal Rights.*

**Partial biographies** cover only a small aspect of the person's life. They focus on specific events and can be very detailed. They might focus on the most important event in a person's life or only focus on a specific period, such as childhood or the teenage years. Here are some we recommend:

> *The Story of Ruby Bridges,* by Robert Coles
> *Teammates,* by Peter Golenbock
> *A Girl Named Helen Keller,* by Margo Lundell

**Picture book biographies**, much like partial biographies, tend to focus on a small part of a person's life, since they are in picture book format and usually just 32 pages long. They use both pictures and text to tell the subject's life story. Many are written for very young readers, but some of the new picture book biographies are geared toward intermediate and middle school readers.

**Collective biographies** are a collection of biographies on a group of people that have something in common. Their stories are presented in short vignettes that focus on the common theme. The books may center on famous African American women, sports stars, computer engineers, movie stars, scientists, or presidents. Here are some we recommend:

*Adventurous Women: Eight True Stories About Women Who Made a Difference*, by Penny Coleman

*50 American Heroes Every Kid Should Meet*, by Dennis Denenberg and Lorraine Roscoe

*Remember the Ladies: 100 Great American Women*, by Cheryl Harness

We think it would be great if students were exposed to many different kinds of biographies. It would also be empowering to your young readers if you asked them who they would like to read about and began adding your students' choices to your biography/autobiography collection. Review the criteria for evaluating biographies (see Figure 4.2) with students so they may make judgments about the ones you've assigned as well as those they've selected themselves.

## Writing Connections

The writing connection for this unit may seem obvious . . . to have students write biographies. Yes, that would be an essential extension to this theme; however, there are many interesting ways to go about it. The core program outlines several writing projects: a clarification composition, a how-to paragraph, a summary, a speech, and a personal essay. We recommend rather than trying to cram in one writing project per week, you choose one or two projects students can engage in and have time to develop throughout the theme. We describe two writing projects that incorporate biographies, as well as autobiographies, in an authentic and engaging way.

## Writing Extension 1: Collective Class Biographies

For this extension, we envision opportunities for students to engage in the decision-making process as they create a class book, perhaps even a collection of biographies. At this point, students have explored the genre so they can simultaneously read and take notes on what makes a really great biography. For the class book, students need to decide on the theme, layout, style, purpose, and audience for the book. To do so, they need to be familiar with a wide variety of collective biographies, and have made note of their different styles, layouts, and themes. Small groups, pairs, or individuals could make a proposal for the themes and structure for the book. Here are possible themes students could choose:

Children Who Have Made a Difference

People in Our Lives Who Are Amazing

Leaders in Our Community

Our Class

Mothers, Fathers, and Siblings

People Who Have Made a Difference in Our Lives

Inventors of Gadgets That Have Changed Our Classroom and Lives

Authors and Illustrators We Love

Someone We Want to Be When We Get Older

Amazing Pets

Celebrities We Look Up To and Those We Don't

We certainly could just assign a topic, but when students have choice they *own* the idea which, in turn, is hugely motivating. You might share as a mentor text one of the numerous collective biographies that are available. Scan some of the layouts from a book and put them up on an overhead projector, so students can examine and decide which design is best for their own writing topic.

When students have completed their writing, it can be published in a class book, with everyone in the class getting a copy. Another option is to publish their work online. Don't be stressed by this choice, as there are many models on the Web to help you (see biography.com for more ideas). Celebrate with your students when they are finished. There is nothing better than a good book and some snacks! Enjoy!

## Writing Extension 2: Multigenre Autobiography

Multigenre writing is another exciting way to engage students in authentic and meaningful writing. It allows you and your students to explore various genres within one project. Too often, students' writing is focused on only one genre at a time. By combining genres into one project, writing becomes an illumination and exploration of self in which students have an opportunity to develop their craft through the writing of various, complementary genres.

In multigenre writing, students write pieces in different genres that all share a unifying theme (Youngs & Barone, 2007). We suggest having students create three to four pieces of writing focusing on the theme of Self. There are a number of ways to organize this project. One way is to organize it around past, present, and future. Students explore events or aspects of their lives from the past, discuss what is important to them right now, and dream of future accomplishments. Each piece of writing provides a window into who your students are. Each genre allows students to show something about themselves that a biography or an autobiography report could not. At the end of the autobiography project students share a much fuller picture of who they are and who they want to be.

Figure 4.3 offers some suggested genres and topics to explore for this project. Any one of them would be appropriate.

## Figure 4.3: GENRE LISTS

| | TOPIC | GENRE |
|---|---|---|
| **PAST** | School | Scrapbook |
| | Babyhood | Birth announcement |
| | Stories from parents | Photo book with captions |
| | Travels | Photo book or brochure |
| | Birthday parties | Invitations |
| **PRESENT** | Sports | Poetry |
| | Friends | Autobiography |
| | Family | Biography of family member |
| | Hobbies | Scrapbook |
| | Parties | Recipe/recipe book |
| | Arts and crafts | Song |
| | Travels | Pamphlets |
| | Class trips | Picture book |
| | Holidays | Advice columns |
| | Plays/drama | E-mail/Web site |
| **FUTURE** | Jobs | TV report |
| | Friends | Autobiography |
| | Family | Résumé |
| | Hobbies | Interview |
| | Parties | Recipe/recipe book |
| | Arts and crafts | Song/poetry |
| | Travels | Pamphlets |
| | College | College diploma |
| | Holidays | Job report |
| | Interests | MySpace page |

Classroom management for this type of project is very important. Teachers need to explicitly teach as many genres as possible and bring in numerous mentor texts. If students are not familiar with genre choices, they might become frustrated and disruptive. You will need to encourage and support students working independently while you work with small groups or individuals who need your guidance for writing. At the end of the project, students can bind together their three to five pieces, along with an introduction, to form their multigenre autobiography.

It's important for students to first think about the important topics and events in their lives that they would like to write about. Then they can think about which genres would provide the best structures for telling that story. The more genres students are familiar with, the easier it'll be for them to find the right ones to tell their stories.

## Author or Illustrator Study

Another way to investigate biographies is through an author/illustrator study. One person we recommend is David Adler, a former math teacher who has written close to 150 books for children. He prefers to write informational books, biographies, and novels. He has written a series of picture book biographies for younger readers, the Picture Book Biography Series (Holiday House). He has also written about the Holocaust and heroes that emerged from that horrific time in history.

To begin the author study, we recommend exposing students to as many of Adler's books as possible. Allow a few days for students to read and share books with one another. At the end of reading time, you might ask students what they noticed about Adler as an author and how different illustrators have envisioned his work. Begin a chart that highlights ideas they have about his books. Also, as a class, do some research on him to find out why he writes biographies and how he conducts his research. Here are some Web sites that provide interesting background

### DAVID ADLER BOOKS

*Our Golda: The Story of Golda Meir*

*A Picture Book of Abraham Lincoln*

*A Picture Book of Anne Frank*

*A Picture Book of Benjamin Franklin*

*A Picture Book of Harriet Tubman*

*A Picture Book of George Washington*

*A Picture Book of John F. Kennedy*

*A Picture Book of John Hancock*

*A Picture Book of Martin Luther King, Jr.*

*A Picture Book of Sacagawea*

information: www.davidaadler.com and http://usawrites4kids.drury.edu/authors/adler/. These sites have lists of books, biographies, and video interviews with him. We think it would be interesting to begin with a read-aloud of the first biography he wrote, *Our Golda: The Story of Golda Meir*, and his most recent biography, *A Picture Book of John Hancock*. Comparing and contrasting his writing over 22 years should prove to be quite illuminating. David Adler is a great children's author, and an author study will provide you and your students with personal insight into the life of a writer.

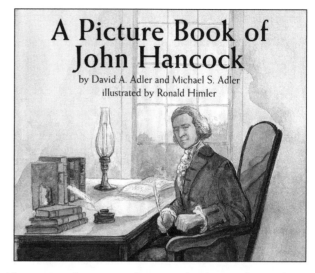

## Ties to Content Areas Such as Social Studies and Science

Exploring biography and autobiography helps students better understand the people they read about in their social studies and science texts. This connection is an easy one for teachers to enact. Working on cooperative biographies or exploring speeches of famous people to learn about them and the times they lived in make for more complex connections.

### Cooperative Biographies

A comprehensive project that integrates social studies and the language arts is the Cooperative Biography created by Walter Parker (2005). You and your students learn cooperatively about a historical figure. Students could choose from presidents, writers, inventors, war heroes, villains, scientists, explorers, social activists, and various leaders around the world. The whole class studies this one person in depth. After conducting preliminary research, the class breaks up into cooperative groups. These groups continue to research and, eventually, collectively write a biography of the chosen historic figure.

The key to this project is explicit instruction on the central events in the person's life, as well as guiding your students to help them interpret the historical evidence presented by various primary and secondary sources. As students are exposed to numerous picture books and other types of biographies, they decide on the format, structure, and design for *their* group biography. This assignment could easily be connected to science if your targeted person were a scientist, thus supporting knowledge of the person behind the scientific discovery.

## Analysis of Famous Speeches

Instead of having children read all five of the speeches provided in the anthology of the core reading program, let them sign up for the one they are most interested in reading. Have them write down their first and second choices and organize them into groups based on their choices. Once you've formed the groups, have students read their group's speech independently or in pairs, marking ideas, questions, and connections they might have about it. Then have the group come back together to discuss the speech and their interpretation of it. You could use a comparison chart or some sort of questionnaire about each speech (see Figure 4.4 for an example). Ask students what aspects of the speech they would like to focus on for discussion so they get a better understanding of the speech genre.

### Figure 4.4: SPEECH GENRE QUESTIONNAIRE

What is the purpose of the speech?

Who is the audience?

What interesting language do you notice?

What are the opening/closing words of the speech?

What impact do you think the opening and closing had?

What is memorable about this speech?

What is the style of this speech?

How did the speaker connect with his/her audience?

Do you think the speaker influenced the audience in any way? Explain.

Who was not addressed in the speech?

What were some of the techniques the speech maker used?

What was the speech maker trying to say?

As an extension of this activity, you could turn the speeches into a Readers Theater. Students might even choreograph the reading so that it is in many voices. For example, in Martin Luther King Jr.'s, "I Have a Dream" speech, there are many places where all students could recite "I have a dream," and then alternate reciting various segments of the speech. Performing the speech as a Readers Theater requires students to focus on the technique of the speaker and on important words that need to be highlighted. Students are given ample time to learn about the speaker, read and analyze the speech, and make critical decisions about how to perform it. The repeated readings certainly impact their fluency as well. A strong resource for speeches is *Words That Built a Nation* (Miller, 1999). The book contains many famous speeches throughout American history. Additionally, many famous speeches can be found in online digital archives (see chart below).

Numerous sites such as these offer access to the text as well as to video and audio clips of historic speeches, providing ties to technology. Seeing the speech allows students to analyze the physical mannerisms and nonverbal communication that are so important to speechmaking.

## ON-LINE DIGITAL SPEECH ARCHIVES

| | |
|---|---|
| www.history.com/media.do | This site, part of the History Channel's Web site, has speeches in a variety of categories. |
| http://famousquotes.me.uk/speeches | This Web site has an extensive collection of famous speeches. Categories include presidential speeches, speeches made by women, and famous speeches from history. |
| www.americanrhetoric.com | The American Rhetoric Web site has created a list of its top 100 speeches of all time. Video and audio clips are available for many of the speeches. |
| www.historyplace.com/speeches | This Web site provides the complete text to a number of famous speeches from history; audio clips are included for many of them, as well. |

## Vocabulary Extensions

For our first vocabulary extension, we recommend that students create personal dictionaries. Students collect interesting words they would like to use in their own writing, unfamiliar words, and words from texts read aloud as well as from their independent reading books. They record them in their personal dictionaries and mark the books with sticky notes. They also use sticky notes to mark any words in their books that they want to learn more about. During read-alouds, students could attend to the language of the text and write interesting words or phrases in their personal dictionaries. Later, several of these words could be placed on a word wall. Such a read-aloud activity works to enhance their listening skills as well.

Secondly, we recommend a theme word wall. Typically, teachers select all the words; we suggest students also be able to offer words. Provide a variety of categories: persuasive words, words found in adversity biographies, words that are interesting, words used routinely in certain genres. You can also put up the vocabulary words from the text and/or have students share words they would like to learn more about. As you can see, we are big on empowering students and giving them a voice wherever possible. We feel they attend to the language more if they have a personal interest in exploring words.

## Visual Literacy Extensions and Technology Connections

### Extension 1: Propaganda and Image

One of the targeted skills listed in the core program is for readers to understand the nature of propaganda. Students are to realize how words and ideas can influence a person's thinking. It is critical for young readers to recognize these techniques in the text and images they encounter on a regular basis. Propaganda is not a thing of the past; it is alive and well in the magazines, TV shows, and texts they read every day. For examples of propaganda techniques that are useful to students' understanding, visit http://propaganda.mrdonn.org.

As an extension into visual literacy, we suggest a unit on image as propaganda. In these activities, students analyze images found in a variety of contexts—such as magazines, TV, video games, and textbooks—and look for ways they might be considered persuasive. It is important for students to understand propaganda as a technique that can be used for positive as well as negative effects. You might compare WWII propaganda posters with Iraq war propaganda posters and look for similarities as well as differences. You might look for propaganda images from the same historical era as the speeches they've selected. Thinking about the civil rights movement, what images were present during that time? You might ask students to think about the power of this poster of Rosa Parks, at right, and how she became a civil rights icon. How did this image impact public perception? What is the context of this photo? What don't we know about this photo? These are all crucial questions to ask, because students typically think of images as snapshots of reality. Students could also look at this famous photo of a migrant mother and her children, taken by Dorothea Lange,

Rosa Parks

Migrant Mother

and ask similar questions. The most important aspect of analyzing propaganda is to place the image or text within a context, whether it be historical or of the current times.

## Extension 2: Multimodal Multigenre Autobiography

Another visual literacy extension would be to turn students' multigenre autobiographies into a digital project. They can use PowerPoint or some similar program to create a digital presentation. Students could focus on the use of color, line, and image placement to enhance their story. They could add audio to the presentation—reading passages of their stories and even overlaying them with music. The possibilities are truly endless. What makes this a visual literacy extension rather than just another presentation is its attention to design elements. You need to facilitate a few lessons on various design elements for children to consider when they're designing their projects.

Kress and van Leeuwen (1996) describe how design elements impact our perceptions in a multitude of ways. For example, colors suggest various emotional responses. Blue can suggest being restful and calm or create a sense of detachment, serenity, or melancholy. Yellow can suggest happiness; red might suggest warmth, anger, energy, or passion.

Attending to the placement of an image has a powerful effect on both the image and the entire design as well. Placing images at the top of page can imply freedom, happiness, or triumph. Placing them at the bottom of a page signifies greater pictorial weight and down-to-earthness, or may even communicate a quality of being threatened. Placement center stage suggests importance, and the larger the picture, the stronger it feels. Students can make important adjustments to their digital multigenre autobiographies with only a few simple ideas to help them to understand the language of image. We feel that visual literacy is critically important in the lives of young readers, as images have become more prominent in their daily lives (Kress, 2003).

# Connections to Sixth-Grade Literacy Standards

This unit meets the following International Reading Association and National Council of Teachers of English standards: Standards 1, 2, 3, 4, 5, 6, 7, 8, 11, and 12.

For this theme, we chose to look at the Nevada English language arts standards, which can be found at www.doe.nv.gov/standards/standela/english.html. The following is an overview of the goals for students in the sixth grade in the state of Nevada (Nevada Department of Education, 2007):

- expand reading comprehension skills using structural analysis
- expand their vocabulary and knowledge of words through context, word study, and multimedia resources
- read and comprehend grade-appropriate text with fluency and expand their use of reading strategies and skills across content areas
- use the writing process to compose a variety of multi-paragraph texts with an awareness of audience and purpose
- revise drafts and then edit for mechanics, word usage, and sentence structure
- formulate questions, research a topic, and write multi-paragraph text to inform or persuade; students also write summaries
- publish their work
- participate in and sometimes lead group discussions
- expand active listening skills and demonstrate public speaking techniques

The majority of these standards were met by the core program and extensions described in this chapter. The reading and writing standards are further broken down into the categories of word analysis, reading strategies, literary text, expository text, effective writing, types of writing, and listening and speaking. Below are some of the strategies covered by the core program and extension activities.

### Standard 1.0, Word Analysis

Students know and use word analysis skills and strategies to comprehend new words encountered in text and to develop vocabulary.

### Standard 2.0, Reading Strategies

Students use reading process skills and strategies to build comprehension to recall details, restate main ideas, organize information, synthesize text, and evaluate text.

### Standard 4.0, Expository Text

Students evaluate information from illustrations, graphs, charts, etc. They explain the use of bold-faced words, underlined words, etc.

### Standard 5.0, Effective Writing

Students write a variety of texts using the writing process. They use prewriting strategies to plan written work, choose and narrow a topic to organize ideas, explore a topic to plan written work, use prewriting strategies to plan written work, draft multiple-paragraph papers about a single topic, draw or write to communicate, and edit essays and compositions to ensure correct spelling of high-frequency words and content words.

### Standard 6.0, Types of Writing

Students write a variety of texts that inform, persuade, describe, evaluate, entertain, or tell a story and are appropriate to audience and purpose and that include topic sentences, details, and concluding statements.

### Standard 7.0, Speaking/Listening

Students listen to and evaluate oral communications for content, style, speaker's purpose, and audience appropriateness. Students speak using organization, style, tone, voice, and media aids appropriate to audience and purpose. Students participate in discussions to offer information, clarify ideas, and support positions.

We have connected the core reading program and extended literacy curriculum to national and state standards. By analyzing the core program, you can determine how well the program supports standards and where you might need to extend it further. The extension of theme and reading and writing practices gives readers time to investigate themes, genres, and text selections in depth. This provides students with multiple opportunities to deepen their understanding of various genres and the purposes of each.

# CHAPTER 5

# $\mathcal{Q}$uestions to Guide the Process of Using Both

*eachers who motivate extensive and effective reading practice among students know how to provide a wide range of high-quality books and other reading materials. Quality, variety, difficulty level, and quantity all matter in a classroom library. Materials need to be interesting, engaging, and appropriately challenging.*
                        —Dorothy S. Strickland and Catherine Snow (2002)

Throughout this book we have shared ways to blend the art and science of reading instruction. Similar to Berliner (1986), we understand that expert teaching requires teachers who use a dynamic mix of expertise on effective strategies, understanding of the expectations for instruction, knowledge of children's literature, and knowledge about the strengths and needs of individual students within a class. We also know that effective teachers are pragmatists who want to know about the nuts and bolts of teaching, especially when they're adding a new dimension to their repertoire. They require efficient support so they can protect the cognitive and creative energy they need to address learning expectations for their students. With that in mind, we wrote this chapter to provide you with that nuts-and-bolts support. We organized this chapter around the questions teachers have asked us about using both.

## "How" Questions

### How does an intermediate teacher find the time to use both?

The daily instructional expectations for you as an intermediate teacher are huge. In addition to providing an extensive curriculum in multiple subjects, you're expected to prepare students to do well on high-stakes assessments. As a result, to use both successfully, you must use the literacy block creatively, making sure it addresses other content requirements. For instance, in Chapter 2, students learned about science content writing an adventure story and a journal with detailed information about a national park. These activities targeted writing and science expectations and provided opportunities for extensive reading and thinking. You can relax a bit knowing that in the two literacy blocks, students are learning important content, developing as readers and writers, and preparing for high-stakes assessments.

To find the time, you first scrutinize your daily schedules and all transition events. (This is most effective if grade-level teachers work together to discover opportunities to increase classroom time.) You may discover that with faster transitions, you can reclaim about 15 minutes per day. Another way to find time is to evaluate activities that do not require teacher guidance and move them to independent practice. For instance, some teachers who required students to write in journals daily moved this activity to independent work and found an additional 15 or 20 minutes. Other teachers decided on the focus of the second block and overlaid it onto other content areas. For example, if students were learning to write an adventure, it became part of the writing block, or if students were creating a brochure about an animal, while tied to science, it became part of the second literacy block. Most teachers tried to find about 45 minutes for the additional block but were initially satisfied with a daily half-hour block as a starting place. They knew that most of the activities students worked on during the second block required complex thinking and would be continued over several days. That freed them from the need to "get it done before the bell rings," making it possible for them to use a relatively small block of time productively.

## How does a teacher begin planning for the use of both?

We recommend that you start with your state and district language arts and content standards and then consider national standards. State and district standards serve as the foundation for teaching and learning expectations for you and your students within each grade level. As we saw in chapters 2, 3, and 4, the standards are often quite broad. For instance, one of Michigan's standards asked students to identify and describe the structure, elements, and purpose of a variety of narrative genres, including poetry, myths, legends, fantasy, and adventure. This standard offers you great leeway in choosing from a multitude of strategies for approaching children's literature.

Next, we recommend that you first explore your core reading program, since the core is often a requirement. Begin with the theme, then scrutinize the text selections and expectations included in the teacher's edition. As we engaged in this process, we listed all of the main text selections and their respective genres. Then we chose a well-written text in a genre that offered numerous opportunities to tie to other curricular areas. Over successive themes, we made sure to vary genres that students became familiar with many of them, even those they did not choose for independent reading.

Text selection can be stressful, especially the first time you do it. It helps to work with grade-level colleagues during a time when you're free of teaching responsibilities. Teachers we know often begin this process on a Saturday morning at one teacher's home with comfort food handy. By beginning this process in a joyful and collegial setting away from the immediate demands of teaching, you may find that it contributes to your growth, rather than adding to your burdens.

As with all teaching, not every selection that you or a group of teachers chooses as a bench-mark text will turn out be the best choice for students at a particular time. While it may be frustrating when the text selection and supporting activities do not accomplish all of your learning goals, keep in mind that no selection is etched in stone and in the future you'll better be able to judge the needs of your students. In subsequent years, you'll have the opportunity to reconsider your selection. You may select a different text and once again move through the creative process of developing activities for your students' reading, writing, and content knowledge growth. The good news is that when this happens, you build a wider repertoire to choose from in subsequent years.

## How should teachers work with their core reading program?

In making instructional decisions, first consider the guidelines of your district and school. Typically, teachers are required to use core reading programs for a daily 90-minute block of instruction. Within this block, you instruct students as a whole group and in small, differentiated groups. The goals of this intermediate-grade instruction center on phonics (although often they are more focused on analysis of words or their roots), fluency, comprehension, and vocabulary.

You begin the decision making for reading instruction through these processes.

- **Exploring the theme.** You review the core text selections, leveled text choices, learning expectations, and support activities to determine how to engage students in instruction and practice.
- **Targeting learning expectations.** You select the most important learning expectations and decide how you will address them. For instance, you may use a text as a model if students are expected to understand character development, or you may select a graphic organizer to help students with comparison.

- **Refining the details.** You revisit the expectations for a week's worth of instruction and estimate the approximate time it will require, as well as the delivery mode. For instance, we suggest that you consider all of the questions that accompany a core-reading text selection and determine which best extend your students' learning. We often find that programs include too many questions. If you use them all, they interrupt the reading so much that students struggle with comprehension. You also need to bring a critical eye to worksheet support. Many of the work sheets are not critical to student learning. They are provided to give you a range of materials to choose from to best meet the needs of students.

- **Reflecting.** You evaluate how each lesson builds to the next. If your students haven't mastered an aspect necessary for understanding, you reteach it. For example, when we noticed that some students needed more time developing inferential understanding of informational text, we created graphic organizer support that enabled students to think more inferentially about text. Importantly, you use the core reading program materials to best support the literacy learning needs of your students.

Because the literacy needs of intermediate students are closely tied to fluency, comprehension, and vocabulary, you'll want to provide for independent practice that supports their growth in these areas. When you work with small, differentiated groups of students, other students typically engage in the following independent work:

**Rereading text.** Students may reread their current leveled text selection or previous leveled text selections independently. After reading three of these books (or whatever number you decide on), they read to a partner. If the target is fluency, the partner might time the student's reading rate (in words per minute). If the target is comprehension, students might share an important part of the plot with a partner or in a written response. If the target is vocabulary, students might share an interesting word and find out what it means or find other similar words.

**Writing about text.** When students write thoughtfully about what they've read, their comprehension deepens. On most occasions you'll ask students to write about something specific, such as three things that are important about a character and the significance of each. We offer more suggestions for writing about text later in this chapter.

**Word study.** Students explore a word pattern, affix, or root. They find other words to fit a pattern, or the teacher provides the words. See Figure 5.1 for an example of a possible word study activity. For additional word study ideas, refer to the core reading program or *Words Their Way* (Bear, Invernizzi, Templeton, & Johnston, 2007) or *Word Journeys* (Ganske, 2000).

**Listening center.** Students struggling with reading benefit from listening to the core reading selection or leveled text at a listening center. Through this additional support, students can participate in whole-class or small-group discussions on the text.

Each of these activities provides for extensive reading, writing, and thinking, even when students are not working directly with you.

## Figure 5.1: WORD STUDY EXAMPLE

Find words that have a prefix that means "not." Write these words. Sort them by prefix. Why do you think there are so many different prefixes for "not"?

unable, disconnect, misspell, unfair, incorrect, nonfat, disobey, unclear, dislike, invisible

| un- | dis- | in- | non- | mis- |
|-----|------|-----|------|------|
| unable | disconnect | incorrect | nonfat | misspell |
| unclear | disobey | invisible | | |
| unfair | dislike | | | |

I have no idea why there are so many prefixes for "not." I don't think I found them all. I tried using un- in front of them all and they sound funny, like unfat. Maybe the sound is a reason for so many different prefixes.

## How should teachers work with their literature block?

Like the core reading block, the literature block in the intermediate grades is guided by standards and learning expectations. What is different here is that you use additional literature to support students' development of comprehension, vocabulary, fluency, and content knowledge. There are two parts to planning this block: selecting appropriate literature and developing activities and strategies for students to use.

Fortunately, there are many places to seek out quality children's literature. We always begin in our school. We check our room, the school's book closet, and the school library to find books related to our theme and to find any other titles by the author(s) or illustrator(s) of the selected text. Colleagues are another rich source of recommendations for titles related to our theme. We also check school book club order forms, like those from Scholastic, to see what might be available to support the theme or other targeted instruction.

Then we visit the Internet. On the opposite page are some of the sites that have proven helpful with the selection of books, magazines, and articles to support instruction.

We also explored print and electronic journals that offer information about books or potential activities or strategies. Below are several of our choices.

### PRINT AND ELECTRONIC RESOURCES FOR TEACHING READING

| | |
|---|---|
| *The Reading Teacher* | This journal is published by the International Reading Association. Each issue contains a section devoted to children's literature. The journal also publishes students', teachers', and parents' choices from newly published children's trade books. (www.reading.org) |
| *Language Arts* | Published by the National Council of Teachers of English, this journal devotes a section in each issue to children's literature. (www.ncte.org) |
| *Book Links* | This journal, published by the American Library Association (www.ala.org), focuses on children's literature. It provides thematic collections of children's books. (P.O. Box 1347, Elmhurst, IL 60126) |
| *Read·Write·Think* | This site, cosponsored by the International Reading Association and the National Council of Teachers of English, features books with lesson plans targeted to specific content and/or literacy strategies. An article with research support and Internet resources is included with each lesson. |

## WEB SITE RESOURCES FOR TEACHING READING

| | |
|---|---|
| www.carolhurst.com | This site has a newsletter about children's books. Many of the books are organized by theme or curricular area. |
| www.ala.org | The American Library Association's Web site provides links to numerous sites dedicated to children's literature. It provides information about the Newbery winners. |
| www.udel.edu/dssep/ literature.html | This site has information about books, grouped by theme, related to social studies topics and themes. |
| www.cloudnet.com/~edr bsass/edchildrenslit.htm | This site offers multiple plans and resources targeted to specific children's books. Teachers may find ideas for activities for their literacy block. |
| www.geocities.com/heart-land/estates/4967/math.html | This site offers 100 top children's books geared to math concepts. They are arranged by topic, such as addition or subtraction. |
| www.childrenslit.com | This site provides information about authors and illustrators. There are suggestions for theme explorations as well. We enjoyed reading through the ideas for using picture books with intermediate readers. |
| www.scholastic.com | This site provides children's books and activities to use with students. We read a sample chapter from *The Land of Elyon: Into the Mist* by Patrick Carman and viewed the author's notes and work that was not included in the print edition of the book. There were also several interesting visual images from the book that we enlarged and perused. We spent time reading about the author's visits to various schools through his journal entries and photos. In connection with Chapter 2, we found information here about Gordon Korman and read sample chapters in his new trilogy about being the youngest climber of Everest. These Internet *expeditions* allow students to gain additional insights into authors and books, thus sustaining and expanding motivation and comprehension. |

Once you've selected your books, brainstorm possible activities for students. To help with this process, we use the following template:

- Reading Connections (Fiction and Nonfiction)
- Writing Connections
- Author or Illustrator Studies
- Extension of Core Theme
- Vocabulary Extensions
- Fluency
- Visual Literacy Extensions
- Connections to Technology

This template is flexible rather than fixed—items can be added or deleted. We use it as a guide during the creative process. Once we have activities in each area, we scrutinize our choices and decide which best support student learning.

# "What" Questions

We find that "what" questions about using both a core reading program and children's literature support our creative instincts as teachers. Because we worry that intermediate students will lose their excitement for reading and writing, and we want to ensure that they are involved in learning, we spend time considering engagement strategies to keep all students focused on instruction (Flint, 2008). To this end, we include two lists for your consideration: literacy strategies and engagement strategies. Additionally, we share many ways that students might write about reading during the literacy block. These strategies all support learning and, in particular, facilitate fluency, word knowledge, comprehension, and vocabulary.

## Literacy Strategies
- **Predicting.** This strategy asks students to refer to the cover of a text or to illustrations to make predictions about the events of a story (Kelley & Clausen-Grace, 2007). Teachers can also use prediction with informational text. Students preview the text, charts, bold print, and so on to narrow the focus for reading. One issue with predicting is that sometimes students think that the point of the strategy is to come up with a "right" prediction and avoid a "wrong" one. This can be a problem particularly with narrative, where authors are free to

create their text with surprising elements. It is better for students to compare their predictions with what happened and have opportunities to revise their ideas.

- **Summarizing**. Students summarize a portion of text by sharing the essential parts (Keene & Zimmermann, 1997). Summarization is a difficult task for students—they are not sure which details to include or ignore. We've found that using the word *important* helps students with summaries. We ask them to tell us the most important part or the most important thing about the character.

- **Think-aloud**. The teacher models her thinking while reading to students (Wilhelm, 2001), showing how she goes about comprehending text. We have seen teachers use this strategy in whole-class or small groups where they stop reading and share their thinking process. There is a brief discussion and then reading continues.

- **Questioning**. Students or the teacher pose questions about what is being read (Searfoss et al., 2001). Students reread or seek help from other sources for clarification. Teachers often provide sticky notes for students to use to record their questions at the puzzling spots in their books. When the teacher convenes a small reading group, students discuss their questions and try to find solutions to support comprehension.

- **Visualizing**. Students create a quick sketch to support comprehension (Wilhelm, 2001). In one classroom, a small group of students was reading *Danny, the Champion of the World* (Dahl, 2007). They were not sure about the caravan that Danny lived in, so their teacher asked them to carefully read the details about the caravan and then do a quick sketch of it to support comprehension.

- **Clarifying**. This process is similar to questioning (Searfoss et al., 2001). Students may need to reread to determine exactly what is happening in a plot. They may need to discuss with a teacher or other students a point of confusion from the reading.

## Engagement Strategies

Keeping students engaged is among a teacher's most important tasks. Without engagement, there is little or no learning. When we observe classrooms with engaged students, there are partner, small-group, and whole-group active discussions. Students write and talk about reading and ideas. We see energy on the part of the teacher and students (Marzano, 2007). The following are several ways to engage students in learning.

- **Buddy buzz**. Students are broken up into partners, with each identified either by letter or number. The teacher asks a question and either Partner A or B responds. For instance, in a class that's working on vocabulary for an upcoming text selection, the teacher might say, "Partner A, tell B three reasons why someone could be *exhilarated.*" After Partner A responds, the teacher requests, "Partner B, share with A three reasons why someone would not be *exhilarated.*" By giving each partner a specific task, we ensure that both contribute and that one doesn't dominate the conversation.

- **Numbered heads.** Students are placed in groups of four or five. Each student has a number. The teacher asks a question, and students in each group work together to find a solution. For instance, we asked groups to find five details from a story they had read in their core program. The group works together for a period of time. Then, the teacher is free to call on any number and that student reports on the work of the group. We found that if each student writes during group work, all students are prepared to answer.

- **Choral response.** The teacher asks a question and signals for students to think about a response for a period of time. Then, all students respond together. For instance, the teacher may say, "I am thinking of a word-wall word that begins with *b* and has a long-*o* pattern in it." The students respond, "*Boat.*"

- **Writing chain**. Students are placed in groups of four or five. The teacher asks them to accomplish a writing task. For instance, the  teacher might say, "Write a synonym for the word *heavy*" or "Write a detail from this story" or "Write a word that describes this character." When students are finished, they pass their papers to the right and the task is repeated. This process continues until each paper returns to its owner. Then students share what they discovered from the various responses.

## Writing During Either Block

Writing helps students stay engaged and deepens comprehension, vocabulary, word knowledge, and fluency when they are working independently. You may wonder what kinds of writing are best for students during the core reading block. If, for example, you want students to deepen comprehension, we recommend that you engage them in focusing on the ideas in their writing, rather than worrying about spelling, grammar, or punctuation. The focus of this writing is thinking, and therefore revision or editing is not a priority. Sometimes you'll find the mistakes distracting, but we suggest that you focus on ideas. You may also find that with increased practice, students spell more conventionally, improve their grammar, and reduce the number of punctuation errors. These elements of writing are certainly important but are better dealt with when students are writing text that will be revised and edited.

During the block, you might ask students to do any of the following.

- **Complete a word sort.** Students find words that fit a pattern chosen by either the teacher or students (see example in Figure 5.1) and then sort them. Students gain word knowledge through this activity, and gain fluency through rereading the text numerous times.

- **Find special words.** Similar to word sorting, this activity asks students to find words from their reading that are descriptive or interesting in some way. Then they work with a partner and find other words that are similar. For example, students may locate words that describe the size of characters or things. Once they find 10 or 15 of these words, the teacher may ask them to discuss their perception of the relative size suggested by each word and then rank them from smallest to largest. When disagreements arise over which word represents a larger object or quantity (e.g., whether a *giant* tree is bigger than an *enormous* one), the students defend their rankings. These activities work on expanding the nuances of vocabulary and fluency through rereading.

- **Use graphic organizers.** Graphic organizers serve to deepen student's comprehension as they read. The organizer should match the structure of the text. Timelines work well for information that is organized chronologically. Webs work well for descriptive information. T-charts or Venn diagrams support comparison writing. A cause-and-effect table works well with texts that address why things happen. A numbered list supports text organized sequentially. For narrative, students might have a chart with columns labeled beginning, middle, and end so that they can provide updated important details about the plot. They might also chart the differences in a character throughout a story. Ideas are endless for this type of writing.

- **Make personal connections.** Students write about personal, text-to-text, or text-to-life connections. Teachers might provide notebooks, sticky notes, or bookmarks for students to record these connections so that they can be shared.

- **Answer questions.** Students reply to higher-level questions. Teachers might ask, for example, that they find three ways the setting contributed to the story.

- **Asking Questions.** Students create three questions (or some number designated by the teacher) that they have about the text. They might answer these questions during small-group time, or they might partner with another student and work together on finding answers.

- **Make lists.** Students create a list, such as "the five most important pieces of information in this text" or "the three best words to describe the character." Students enjoy composing these lists on list-like paper—long and narrow.

## BOOKMARKS

| | | | |
|---|---|---|---|
| When I read this I stopped to think. This is what I read and what I was thinking. | The most important part of my reading is | Something that really confused me was | I think the whole class needs to know the word _____ because |

- **Use bookmarks.** Teachers create bookmarks that students use for recording what they notice and wonder about as they read or for responding to prompts provided by the teacher. Bookmarks give students a place to jot down quick responses as they read. Because they are not as big as a whole sheet of paper, students feel safer writing on them (McLaughlin & Fisher, 2005).

- **Create semantic maps.** Students create a cluster with a topic or important word in the center. If the topic were "frogs," it would appear in the center; the other areas of the map might be labeled "kinds of frogs," "what frogs eat," "the life cycle of the frog," and "enemies of frogs." As students read they complete each of these areas.

- **Create semantic question maps.** The format is the same as for a semantic map except that each area has a question. A map for the rain forest might include these questions: Where are the rainforests? What can we do to save the rain forests? What lives in the rain forest? What grows in the rain forest?

- **Sketch connections.** Students create a quick sketch of their connection to the text and then write several sentences about it. The focus is on the writing—the drawing is a way to engage thinking.

- **Make a double-entry draft.** On a sheet of paper divided into two columns, students copy a portion of text that stands out for them in some way on the left-hand side. On

**Figure 5.2: DOUBLE-ENTRY DRAFT RESPONSE**

| Double-Entry Draft | |
|---|---|
| "On our street, besides the thrift shop, there is a pet shop, a sewing machine shop, an electric shop, a couple of junk shops they call antique shops, plus a taco king and a softee freeze."<br><br>Snyder, Z. (2007) *The Egypt Game.* | I like that sentence because it reminds me of the little town that my Grandma and Grandpa live in. I like to go there it is fun. They have two Parks there and lots of alleys. They have a tricycle as big as a bicycle. It has a basket in the back. I like to ride it to the Park. |

the right, they explain why they selected the text (Barone, 1990). There may be grammatical mistakes, but ignore them for now. This format helps students move toward personal connections to text and away from literal responses. Figure 5.2 is an example of a double-entry draft response by a student who was reading *The Egypt Game* (Snyder, 2007).

# Assessment Issues

These days there's more pressure than ever about students' growth in literacy, so documenting it is particularly important. Because intermediate students' literacy growth can be subtle and difficult to notice, student portfolios are particularly beneficial (Barone & Taylor, 2007). Okay, we hear you groaning. Your previous experiences with portfolios may have convinced you they're labor intensive. Please keep reading, as we think we have streamlined the portfolio process for you by breaking it into two parts. You're already doing the first part—keeping data on students from formal and informal assessments—so take a deep breath here. This part of the process does not change, as such data is needed to plan classroom instruction and for school-wide reform efforts. We offer two ways to build and use student portfolios, one more challenging than the other.

The first method is a broader way to engage in this process and requires sophisticated thinking on the part of students. Students form learning goals for themselves for a particular part of time during the school year. Often the time period is driven by report card or parent conference dates. The teacher provides paper and headings for each major content area and asks students to decide on goals for each of them. For reading, a student might write, "I want to read faster" or "I want to understand better." At first, these goals are large and often not very specific; it takes time and repeated opportunities for students to learn how to write appropriate goals. Then the teacher asks students to write the steps they'll need to take to accomplish their goals. Returning to the goal of wanting to read faster, a student might come up with the following steps: "I am going to read each day for 20 minutes. I am going to time my reading twice each week. I will read with a partner once a week." The goal sheet with detailed steps is stapled to the front of a portfolio (often a file folder or a large piece of construction paper folded in half). Once a week or every two weeks, students place evidence of progress toward their goals in their folders. The teacher may ask students to place sticky notes with an explanation of why the sample is included. For instance, one boy who was working on fluency placed a list of the books he read into his portfolio. He wrote that the list showed he was practicing reading. The reason a piece of work is included is important, as it lets students see how the particular work they do helps them accomplish their learning goals.

In the second method, you select the goals and the students choose the work that documents their growth. For instance, you might decide that students are going to work on comprehending informational text. You create the steps to accomplish this goal: Students will read informational text daily, create graphic organizers to match the text they read, and share important facts from the text they read with partners at least once per week. You determine when students place documentation of their reading goal accomplishments in their portfolio. Once again, they use sticky notes to record their reasons for including each piece of work.

Each of these methods requires students—not you—to select their documentation. In this way, they are responsible not only for learning but also for documenting it. The physical evidence accumulated in portfolios makes visible the more sophisticated learning that occurs in the intermediate grades. Students, teachers, and parents can find times for celebration as they consider the evidence of the complex process of learning—something they may have missed otherwise.

# Getting Started and Continuing

Throughout this book we have offered arguments and evidence to establish the effectiveness of using both a core reading program and literature-based instruction. We have provided details about how to bring both to classrooms, as well as models of what using both might look like. We've suggested how you could meet numerous teaching and learning expectations through the use of both. So now, it is time to start. We know that any change in curriculum requires time to think and reflect about the change, its importance, and ways you will sustain it. We know that as you bring both—core reading programs and literature-based curricula—to your classroom, the moments of joy and exhilaration you see in your students and yourself will be tempered by times of frustration. To support you in those times, we offer a few quotes that have nurtured our spirits during similar times.

- "We teachers need to continue to evaluate how we use our time. First and foremost, we must do whatever we can to ensure that our students love learning. We all invest more energy when a task is pleasurable. Focusing on strengths is the best way to learn anything. Kids can't be joyful if we're not."
  (Regie Routman, 2003, p. 219)

- "When students connect to literature on a personal level, they can begin to understand that they have similar experiences or feelings. This allows them to understand that the everyday occurrences in their lives have meaning and are worth sharing."
  (Lynee Dorfman & Rose Cappelli, 2007, p. 20)

- "Before we can help students learn to read, we have to help them understand why they should read. It is our responsibility as teachers of reading to help novice readers see the value of reading and the wonders of literature. We invite children into the world of reading by experiencing literature together, providing ready access to reading materials, creating time and opportunities for students to read, and supporting students as they share their ideas about their reading with other students."
  (Frank Serafini, 2004, p. 9)

- "Effective teachers are able to differentiate and contextualize their instruction and to support the practices they choose through evidence provided by research and through discussions and collaborations with colleagues in their schools and districts."
  (Linda Gambrell, Lesley Morrow, & Michael Pressley, 2007, p. 16)

- "Good teaching is complicated as well as passionate."
  (Richard Allington & Peter Johnston, 2002, p. 4)

- "Teachers have the power to produce readers who are capable of thinking beyond the level of recognition, recall, and recitation. They have the power to develop readers who think and question, feel and react, and imagine."
(Pamela Dunston, 2002, p. 135)
- "As artists, teachers and students call attention to particular details of the classroom, foregrounding important aspects of the classroom that support literacy and community."
(Margaret Stewart, 2002, p. 177)

So, the time is here. Find a quiet Saturday, invite grade-level colleagues to your home, and begin planning your first use of both. Enjoy the creative process, and then, return to your classroom as an architect: a teacher who uses the science and art of teaching to build student learning and enjoyment.

# $\mathcal{P}$rofessional References Cited

Afflerbach, P. (2007). *Understanding and using reading assessment, K–12*. Newark, DE: International Reading Association.

Allington, R., & Cunningham, P. (2002). *Schools that work where all children read and write* (2nd ed.). Boston: Allyn and Bacon.

Allington, R., & Johnston, P. (2001). Characteristics of exemplary fourth grade instruction. In C. Roller (Ed.), *Research on effective teaching* (pp. 150–165). Newark, DE: International Reading Association.

Allington, R., & Johnston, P. (2002). *Reading to learn: Lessons from exemplary fourth-grade classrooms*. New York: Guilford.

Anderson, N. (2005). *Elementary children's literature: The basics for teachers and parents*. Upper Saddle River, NJ: Allyn & Bacon.

Anstey, M., & Bull, G. (2006). *Teaching and learning multiliteracies: Changing times, changing literacies*. Newark, DE: International Reading Association.

Barone, D. (1990). The written responses of young children: Beyond comprehension to story understanding. *The New Advocate, 3*, 49–56.

Barone, D. (1992). "That reminds me of": Using dialogue journals with young children. In C. Temple & P. Collins (Eds.), *Stories and readers: New perspectives on literature in the elementary classroom* (pp. 85–191). Norwood, MA: Gordon.

Barone, D., Mallette, M., & Xu, S. (2005). *Teaching early literacy*. New York: Guilford.

Barone, D., & Taylor, J. (2007). *The practical guide to classroom literacy assessment*. Thousand Oaks, CA: Corwin Press.

Bear, D., & Barone, D. (1998). *Developing literacy*. Boston: Houghton Mifflin.

Bear, D., Invernizzi, M., Templeton, S., & Johnston, F. (2007). *Words their way* (4th ed.). New York: Prentice Hall.

Berliner, D. (1986). In pursuit of the expert pedagogue. *Educational Researcher, 15*(7), 5–13.

Cochran-Smith, M. (1984). *The making of a reader*. Norwood, NJ: Ablex.

Dillon, S. (2005, October 20). Education law gets first test in U.S. schools. *The New York Times*. Retrieved April 29, 2007, from www.nytimes.com/2005/10/20/national/20exam.html.

Dorfman, L., & Cappelli, R. (2007). *Mentor texts*. Portland, ME: Stenhouse.

Dunston, P. (2002). Instructional components for promoting thoughtful literacy learning. In C. Block, L. Gambrell, & M. Pressley (Eds.), *Improving comprehension instruction* (pp. 135–152). Hoboken, NJ: Jossey-Bass.

Elley, W. (1989). Vocabulary acquisition from listening to stories. *Reading Research Quarterly, 24,* 174–187.

Flint, A. (2008). *Literate lives: Teaching reading and writing in elementary classrooms*. Hoboken, NJ: John Wiley & Sons.

Florio-Ruane, S., & Raphael, T. (2004). Reconsidering our research: Collaboration, complexity, design, and the problem of "scaling up what works." *National Reading Conference Yearbook, 54,* 170–188.

Gambrell, L. (1996). Creating classroom cultures that foster reading motivation. *The Reading Teacher, 52,* 30–40.

Gambrell, L., Morrow, L., & Pressley, M. (2007). *Best practices in literacy instruction* (3rd ed.). New York: Guilford.

Ganske, K. (2000). *Word journeys*. New York: Guilford.

Goodman, K. (1986). *What's whole in whole language?* Richmond Hill, Ontario, Canada: Scholastic.

Hannaway, J., Fix, M., & Passel, J. (2004). The changing demography of urban America. In D. Lapp, C. C. Block, E. J. Cooper, J. Flood, N. Roser, & J. V. Tinajero (Eds.), *Teaching all the children* (pp. 3–11). New York: Guilford.

Hartman, D., & Hartman, J. (1993). Reading across texts: Expanding the role of the reader. *The Reading Teacher, 47,* 202–211.

Haycock, K. (1998). Good teaching matters . . . a lot. *Thinking K–16, 3*(2), 1–14.

Hoffman, J., McCarthey, S., Elliot, B., Bayles, D., Price, D., Ferree, A., & Abbott, J. (1998). The literature-based basals in first grade classrooms: Savior, Satan, or same-old, same-old? *Reading Research Quarterly, 35,* 168–197.

International Reading Association and National Council of Teachers of English (1996). *Standards for the English language arts.* Newark, DE: International Reading Association.

Johnston, P. (2004). *Choice words.* Portland, ME: Stenhouse.

Keene, E., & Zimmermann, S. (1997). *Mosaic of thought: Teaching comprehension in a reader's workshop.* Portsmouth, NH: Heinemann.

Kelley, M., & Clausen-Grace, N. (2007). *Comprehension shouldn't be silent.* Newark, DE: International Reading Association.

Kress, G. (2003). *Literacy in the new media age.* London: Routledge Falmer.

Kress, G., & van Leeuwen, T. (1996). *Reading images: The grammar of visual design.* London: Routledge Falmer.

Ladson-Billings, G. (1994). *The dreamkeepers: Successful teachers of African-American children.* San Francisco: Jossey-Bass.

Lapp, D., Fisher, D., Flood, J., Goss-Moore, K., & Moore, J. (2002). Selecting materials for the literacy program. In S. Wepner, D. Strickland, & J. Feeley (Eds.), *The administration and supervision of reading programs* (3rd ed., pp. 83–94). New York: Teachers College Press.

Marzano, R. (2003). *What works in schools: Translating research into action.* Alexandria, VA: Association of Supervision and Curriculum Development.

Marzano, R. (2007). *The art and science of teaching.* Alexandria, VA: Association for Supervision and Curriculum Development.

McLaughlin, M., & Fisher, L. (2005). *Research-based reading lessons for K–3.* New York: Scholastic.

Michigan Department of Education. (2006). *English language arts grade level content expectations.*

Minnesota Academic Standards Committee. (2003). *Minnesota academic standards: Language arts K–12.* St. Paul, MN: Minnesota Department of Education.

Morrow, L. (1991). Relationships among physical designs of play centers, teachers' emphasis on literacy in play, and children's literacy behaviors during play. In J. Zutell & S. McCormick (Eds.), *Learner factors/teacher factors: Issues in literacy research and instruction—fortieth yearbook of the National Reading Conference* (pp. 127–140). Chicago: National Reading Conference.

National Assessment of Educational Progress. (2005). *The nation's report card.* From the U.S. Department of Education, National Center for Education Statistics Web site: http://nces.ed.gov/nationsreportcard/.

National Center for Education Statistics (2007). *The nation's report card: Reading 2007.* Available at: http://nces.ed.gov/nationsreportcard/reading/results2007.

National Reading Panel. (2000). *Teaching children to read: An evidence-based assessment of the scientific research literature on reading and its implications for reading instruction: Reports of the subgroups.* Washington, DC: National Institute of Child Health and Development.

Nevada Department of Education. (2007). *Nevada English language arts standards: Integrating content and process.*

Newkirk, T. (2003, September 10). The quiet crisis in boys' literacy. *Education Week, 23*(2), 34. Retrieved April 29, 2007, from www.edweek.org/ew/articles/2003/09/10/02newkirk.h23.html.

Obenchain, K., & Morris, R. (2007). *50 social studies strategies for K–8 classrooms.* Upper Saddle River, NJ: Pearson.

Parker, W. C. (2005). *Social studies in elementary education* (5th ed.). Upper Saddle River, NJ: Prentice Hall.

Pearson, P. D., Raphael, T., Benson, V., & Madda, C. (2007). Balance in comprehensive literacy instruction: Then and now. In L. Gambrell, L. Morrow, & M. Pressley (Eds.), *Best practices in literacy instruction* (3rd ed., pp. 30–56). New York: Guilford.

Peterson, R., & Eeds, M. (2007). *Grand conversations: Literature groups in action.* New York: Scholastic.

Popp, H. (1975). Current practices in the teaching of beginning reading. In J. Carroll & J. Chall (Eds.), *Toward a literate society* (pp. 101–146). New York: McGraw-Hill.

Pressley, M. (2006). *Reading instruction that works: A case for balanced teaching.* New York: Guilford.

Pressley, M., Allington, R., Wharton-McDonald, R., Collins-Block, C., & Morrow, L. (2001). *Learning to read: Lessons from exemplary first-grade classrooms.* New York: Guilford.

RAND Reading Study Group. (2001). *Reading for understanding: Toward an R&D program in reading comprehension* (Technical report for the Office of Education Research and Improvement). Santa Monica, CA: RAND.

Raphael, T. E., Pardo, L. S., & Highfield, K. (2002). *Book club: A literature-based curriculum* (2nd ed.). Lawrence, MA: Small Planet Communications.

Routman, R. (2003). *Reading essentials: The specifics you need to teach reading well.* Portsmouth, NH: Heinemann.

Searfoss, L., Readence, J., & Mallette, M. (2001). *Helping children learn to read: Creating a classroom literacy environment.* Boston: Allyn and Bacon.

Serafini, F. (2004). *Lessons in comprehension.* Portsmouth, NH: Heinemann.

Serafini, F., & Serafini-Youngs, S. (2006). *Around the reading workshop in 180 days.* Portsmouth, NH: Heinemann.

Smith, F. (1979). *Reading without nonsense.* New York: Teachers College Press.

Snow, C., Burns, M., & Griffin, P. (Eds.). (1998). *Preventing reading difficulties in young children.* Washington, DC: National Research Council, National Academy Press.

Stahl, S. (1998). Understanding shifts in reading and its instruction. *Peabody Journal of Education, 73,* 31–67.

Stahl, S., & Miller, P. (2006). Whole language and language experience approaches for beginning reading: A quantitative research synthesis. In S. Stahl & M. McKenna (Eds.), *Reading research at work: Foundations of effective practice* (pp. 36–44). New York: Guilford.

Stewart, M. (2002). *"Best practice"? Insights on literacy instruction from an elementary classroom.* Mahwah, NJ: Lawrence Erlbaum.

Strickland, D., & Snow, C. (2002). *Preparing our teachers: Opportunities for better reading instruction.* Washington, DC: Joseph Henry Press.

Taboada, A., Guthrie, J., & McRae, A. (2008). Building engaging classrooms. In R. Fink & S. J. Samuels (Eds.), *Inspiring reading success: Interest and motivation in an age of high-stakes testing* (pp. 141–166). Newark, DE: International Reading Association.

Taylor, B., Pearson, P. D., Clark, K., & Walpole, S. (2000). Effective schools and accomplished teachers: Lessons about primary grade reading instruction in low-income schools. *Elementary School Journal, 101,* 121–165.

Tunnell, M., & Jacobs, J. (2008). *Children's literature, briefly* (4th ed.). Upper Saddle River, NJ: Pearson.

Wilhelm, J. (2001). *Improving comprehension with think-aloud strategies: Modeling what good readers do.* New York: Scholastic.

Worthy, J., Ivey, G., & Broaddus, K. (2001). *Pathways to independence: Reading, writing, and learning in grades 3–8*. New York: Guilford.

Worthy, J., Moorman, G., & Turner, M. (1999). What Johnny likes to read is hard to find in schools. *Reading Research Quarterly, 34*, 12–27.

Youngs, S., & Barone, D. (2007). *Writing without boundaries: What's possible when students combine genres*. Portsmouth, NH: Heinemann.

# $\mathcal{C}$hildren's Literature Cited

Bang, M. (1999). *When Sophie gets angry—really, really, angry*. New York: Blue Sky.

Bradby, M. (1995). *More than anything else*. New York: Scholastic.

Briggs Martin, J. (1998). *Snowflake Bentley*. Boston: Houghton Mifflin.

Browne, A. (1986). *Piggybook*. New York: Alfred A. Knopf.

Browne, A. (2001). *Voices in the park*. New York: DK Publishing.

Bunting, E. (1989). *The Wednesday surprise*. New York: Clarion.

Bunting, E. (1994). *Smoky night*. New York: Clarion.

Clements, A. (2003). *Frindle*. New York: Scholastic.

Craighead, S. (2004). *Bugling elk and sleeping grizzlies*. Guilford, CT: Falcon Guide.

Creech, S. (1994). *Walk two moons*. New York: HarperCollins.

Creech, S. (2001). *Love that dog*. New York: HarperCollins.

Dahl, R. (2007). *Danny, the champion of the world*. New York: Puffin.

dePaola, T. (2000). *Nana upstairs & Nana downstairs*. New York: Puffin.

Domeniconi, D. (2007). *M is for majestic: A national parks alphabet*. Chelsea, MI: Sleeping Bear Press.

Fox, M. (1985). *Wilfrid Gordon McDonald Partridge*. Brooklyn, NY: Kane/Miller.

George, J. C. (1972). *Julie of the wolves*. New York: Harper Trophy.

George, J. C. (1988). *My side of the mountain*. New York: Puffin Books.

Halvorsen, L. (2000). *Letters home from our national parks: Yosemite*. Chicago: Blackbirch Press.

Henkes, K. (1997). *Sun and spoon*. New York: Greenwillow Books.

Henkes, K. (2003). *Olive's ocean*. New York: HarperCollins.

Hermes, P. (2002). *A perfect place: Joshua's Oregon Trail diary*. New York: Scholastic.

Hesse, K. (1999). *Just juice*. New York: Scholastic.

Hughes, L. (1996). *The dream keeper and other poems.* New York: Knopf Books for Young Readers.

Justesen K. (2006). *"Hey ranger!" Kids ask questions about Yellowstone National Park.* Guilford, CT: Falcon Guide.

Korman, G. (2006). *Kidnapped: Book three: The rescue.* New York: Scholastic.

McMullan, K. (2003). *For this land: Meg's prairie diary.* New York: Scholastic.

Miller, M. (1999). *Words that built a nation: A young person's collection of historic American documents.* New York: Scholastic.

Naylor, P. R. (1996). *The fear place.* New York: Aladdin.

Paulsen, G. (2006). *Hatchet.* New York: Aladdin.

Petersen, D. (2001). *National parks.* New York: Children's Press.

Rahaman, V. (1997). *Read for me, mama.* New York: Boyds Mills Press.

Rappaport, D. (2001). *Martin's big words: The life of Dr. Martin Luther King, Jr.* New York: Hyperion Books for Children.

Raschka, C. (1993). *Yo! Yes?* New York: Orchard Books.

Reilly-Giff, P. (2002). *Picture of Hollis Woods.* New York: Scholastic.

Ryan, P. M. (1999). *Amelia and Eleanor go for a ride.* New York: Scholastic.

Ryan, P. M. (2002). *When Marian sang: The true recital of Marian Anderson.* New York: Scholastic.

Say, A. (2004). *Allison.* Boston: Houghton Mifflin.

Snyder, Z. (2007). *The Egypt game.* New York: Atheneum.

Spinelli, J. (2002). *Maniac McGee.* New York: Scholastic.

Spinelli, J. (2000). *Stargirl.* New York: Knopf.

Spinelli, J. (1997). *Wringer.* New York: Harper Trophy.

Viorst, J. (1971). *The tenth good thing about Barney.* New York: Atheneum Books for Young Readers.

Williams, V. (1988). *A chair for my mother.* New York: Mulberry Books.

Winter, J. (2005). *The librarian of Basra: A true story from Iraq.* New York: Harcourt Children's Books.

Yashima, T. (1976). *Crow boy.* New York: Puffin.

# Index

Meunier, Brian, 50

*Michelangelo*, 84

Michigan, fourth-grade literacy standards for, 45–47, 100

Minnesota, fifth-grade literacy standards for, 70–71

*Miss Alaineus: A Vocabulary Disaster*, 50, 54–55, 56, 63–64

Morrow, Lesley, 113

Motivation, 16

Muir, John, 42

Multigenre writing, 63
    for autobiography, 88, 90
    multimodal, 95–96

Music, as response to literature, 63

*My Red Balloon*, 64

*My Side of the Mountain*, 33–34, 40

Myers, Laurie, 29

Narrative text, fourth-grade literacy standards for, 46

National Assessment of Educational Progress (NAEP), 8
    criteria of, 9

National Council of Teachers of English (NCTE), 22, 45

*National Parks*, 37–38

National Parks, Websites about, 45

Nevada, sixth-grade literacy standards for, 96–97

No Child Left Behind Act (NCLB), 9, 19

*No Ordinary Baby: Wolfgang Amadeus Mozart*, 73, 85

Nonfiction, and extended literacy curriculum, 35–38

Numbered heads strategy, 108

*Olive's Ocean*, 58

*One More Flight*, 64

Oral language, in fifth-grade core program, 50

Ortega, Katherine, 73

*Our Golda: The Story of Golda Meir*, 91

Parker, Charlie, 91

Parks, Rosa, 94, 95

Partial biographies, 86

*A Perfect Place: Joshua's Oregon Trail Diary*, 38

Personal connection, in writing, 109

Personal dictionaries, 94

Phonics
    in fifth-grade core program, 51
    in fourth-grade core program, 31
    in sixth-grade core program, 75

Picture book biographies, 86

*A Picture Book of John Hancock*, 91

*A Picture Book of Lewis and Clark*, 84

*Pictures of Hollis Woods*, 57

*Piggybook*, 60

*Pipiolo and the Roof Top Dogs*, 50

Poetry
    anthologies of, 61
    appreciation of, 61–62

Portfolios, 27, 111
    development of, 112

Predicting, 106–107

Presidential Physical Fitness Challenge, 67

Pressley, Michael, 113

Proficient level of reading proficiency, 9

Propaganda, 94–95

Questioning, 107, 109
    vs. discussion, 54, 55
    effective, 106–108

*Read-Write-Think*, 104

Readers' theater, 03

Reading
    fostering love of, 29, 113
    fifth-grade literacy standards for, 70
    rereading, 102
    text selection for, 101
    writing about, 102

Reading comprehension. *See* Comprehension

Reading strategies, sixth-grade literacy standards for, 96

*The Reading Teacher*, 104

Realistic fiction, 56–57
    questions posed by, 64
    resolutions in, 60
    responding to, 62–64
    suggested selections in, 57–58
    text sets in, 59

Reflecting, importance of, 102

*Remember the Ladies: 100 Great American Women*, 87

Rereading texts, 26

Reviews, book, 64

Roosevelt, Eleanor, 84

Roscoe, Lorraine, 87

Routman, Regie, 11, 113

Say, Allen, 29

Schanzer, Rosalyn, 50

Scheduling
    issues in, 20